Rediscovering ancient Greece

ARCHITECTURE AND CITY PLANNING

© Copyright 1999 for I. E. PHOCA - P. D. VALAVANIS, KEDROS PUBLISHERS INC.
First Edition «ΑΡΧΙΤΕΚΤΟΝΙΚΗ ΚΑΙ ΠΟΛΕΟΔΟΜΙΑ», KEDROS 1992

Distributed by Kedros Publishers S.A.
3 Gennadiou St., Athens 106 78
Tel. 38.09.712, 38.02.007 – FAX 38.31.981

ISBN 960-04-1519-6

IOANNA PHOCA and PANOS VALAVANIS

Rediscovering
ancient Greece

ARCHITECTURE AND CITY PLANNING

TRANSLATED BY
TIMOTHY CULLEN

ILLUSTRATED BY
SOPHIA ZARAMBOUKA

3rd edition

KEDROS BOOKS

ACKNOWLEDGEMENTS

Our sincere thanks are due to the following, who have generously allowed us to use their photographs and other material as illustrations in this book: Spyros Baziotopoulos, Christos Doumas, Yorgos Drakopoulos, Katerina Fornié, Hans R. Goette, Herman Kienast, Manolis Korres, Nelly Kouskoleka, Annie Skassi, Elsie Spathari, Stavros and Stella Stavridis, Nikos Tsouchlos, E. Vardala-Theodorou.

We are also most grateful to the following for kindly allowing us to use slides from their collections: Museum of Cycladic and Ancient Greek Art, Kanellopoulos Museum, National Archaeological Museum (Athens), Numismatic Museum (Athens), Hellenic Maritime Museum of Greece (Piraeus), Acropolis Museum, Epigraphical Museum (Athens), and the archives of the Archaeological Receipts Fund, the National Bank of Greece, the French School of Archaeology and the École Nationale Supérieure des Beaux-Arts (Paris).

Lastly, we are indebted to Dinos Kyriakopoulos, who read the final draft of the text and made valuable comments and suggestions, and to Eleftheria Kondylaki for her assistance.

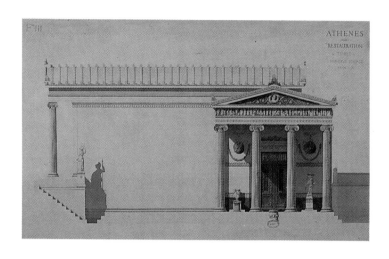

CONTENTS

PAGES

Infrastructure, commerce and defence

Architecture for the afterlife

Religious architecture

Mind and matter

GRAND AVTEL DE ZEVS
DETAIL AV QVART

FOREWORD

The word "architecture" denotes the art and techniques used in the making of structures out of a wide variety of materials for life in this world and the next, and for the worship of the gods.

The art of architecture arose from the need of our primitive ancestors to protect themselves from predators and the elements, especially while they were sleeping. In the course of time it broadened in scope to cover all their activities as their social life developed and they came to require complex buildings, villages, towns, large cities and amenities of various kinds.

The forms of the buildings in use in any particular community are and always have been inseparably linked with the natural environment (position, climate, materials available), the degree of wealth or poverty, the political system in force (monarchy, feudalism, democracy, etc.), the prevailing religious and metaphysical beliefs, and the level of artistic development of the people who built them. All these factors have a direct and lasting effect on the layout of a village, the design of a house or the appearance of a temple façade.

Architecture is one of the earliest manifestations of the human mind and will, and it is the one which most clearly reveals the character, identity and cultural level of the people concerned. It is no accident that so great a variety of architectural forms was produced in ancient Greece, especially in historical times: that very variety reflects the distinctive character, the imaginativeness, the logical mind and the aesthetic taste of the people who conceived those forms. It also hints at the political and social structures they had developed in order to be able to make the most of life while behaving responsibly and creatively both as individuals and as a community. In terms of both architectural and social development, the ancient Greek *polis* or city-state is the crowning achievement of classical civilization – in fact it provides the root of the Greek word for civilization itself, *politismos*.

The masterpieces of Greek architecture of the historical era did not come into being independently of what had been done in prehistoric times: they were the culmination of thousands of years of building development, which was certainly influenced by the architecture of other civilizations in the Mediterranean and the Middle East.

The beginnings

Our ancestors who lived in the Upper Palaeolithic (the period starting *c.* 40,000 B.C.) were hunter-gatherers, that is to say they were constantly on the move from place to place in search of the food that nature provided: animals in their various grazing areas and fruit and nuts that ripened at different times and places. At night they usually slept out in the open, or in caves or other natural shelters.

Between about 10,000 and 7000 B.C., a period of rising temperatures, this way of life gradually changed. Instead of living off the land, human beings learnt how to produce food for themselves by cultivating crops or domesticating certain kinds of animals. One consequence of these newly-acquired skills – and at the same time an essential prerequisite for their development – was that people lived permanently in one place. They now built huts on piles in lakes, to protect themselves from wild animals, or else they constructed houses or communal settlements using stones, bricks, twigs and reeds. In the Neolithic (*c.* 7000-3000 B.C.) we can start talking about architecture, even though the finds from that time amount to no more than the remains of small villages

and built tombs. In Mesopotamia and Palestine, however, some settlements of hunter-gatherers, such as Jericho, grew so big that they can fairly be called towns.

Dimini: a settlement of 5000-3000 B.C.

In Greece, the Neolithic settlements that have been found almost all over the country are small. The richest archaeological finds have come from settlements in Thessaly such as Sesklo, Kranon, Dimini and Tsangli (whose prehistoric names are unknown, so they are named after the nearest modern village or physical landmark).

The settlement of Dimini (1) stands on a hilltop near Volos. It consists of five concentric defensive walls enclosing a village of one-roomed houses, most of which abut on the circuit walls. At the summit there is a flat terrace with a larger, two-roomed house that may have belonged to the ruler. The only surviving remains of the houses are low walls built of rough stones: the upper courses would have been made of unbaked, sun-dried bricks, which have naturally crumbled away with the passage of time. The roofs, too, which were probably made of

wooden beams, branches, reeds and mud, have likewise disintegrated. No tiles have been found anywhere, although the discovery of attractively painted kiln-baked vases (2) proves that the inhabitants of these villages were familiar with the art of pottery. Clay models of houses found in the excavations suggest that the exterior walls of the houses were decorated. The layout of these small Neolithic settlements attests to an equally simple social structure: a community of a fairly small number of families, perhaps with a local ruler. Each settlement would have been economically independent, which means that the inhabitants consumed the crops and livestock products that they themselves had produced.

2

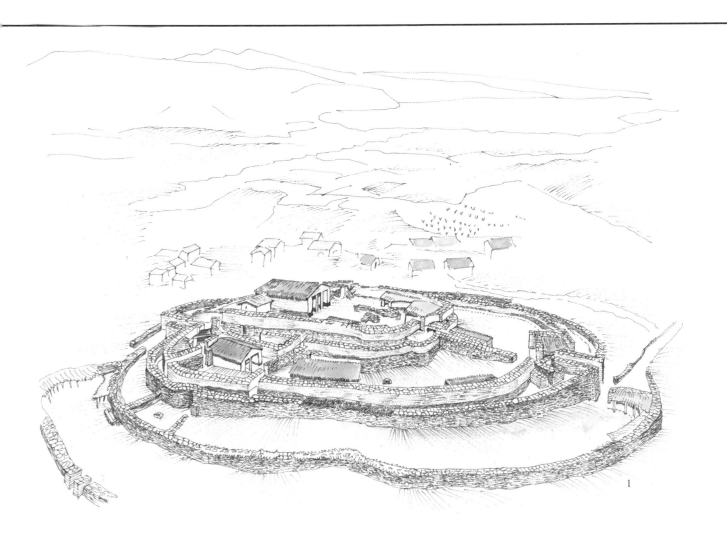

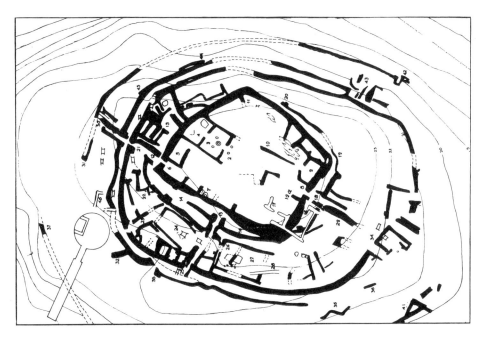

Knossos: a palace and city of 2000-1500 B.C.

In Crete, Neolithic settlements are to be found from about 5000 B.C. onwards. In the Bronze Age, which came next, large buildings were often erected on the rubble of ruined settlements, the most famous of them being the palaces built after 2000 B.C. at Knossos, Phaistos, Zakros and Mallia. About the people who made and lived in these palaces we know nothing more than what is to be learnt from the frescoes found on the walls: that they were slight of build, dark-haired and lightly clad (1). Sir Arthur Evans, the first excavator of Knossos, coined the term "Minoan" – after Minos, the legendary priest-king of Knossos – to describe these people and their civilization. The palace covers an area of about five acres (two hectares) on a levelled hilltop and is surrounded by luxury villas and a small city of dependent buildings. Its position was well chosen to command the sea and the main routes to the surrounding country and the mountains.

All the rooms of the palace, which rose to a height of at least three storeys in some parts, are laid out round a large central courtyard which was presumably used for public meetings and religious ceremonies (2). There were rooms to serve a wide variety of purposes: living quarters for the royal family, ritual chambers, shrines, offices, large storerooms (3) and workshops. All are allotted their proper places in an overall design that testifies to the skill and imaginativeness of the architects. Although the palace was so large and complex that it gave rise to the legend of the labyrinth, its design was functionally efficient. It had ample living accommodation, a system of galleries and roofed verandas that provided natural air conditioning, good natural lighting, a water supply and a drainage system. The large doorways, wide staircases, spacious and lavishly-decorated rooms, balconies and open-air shrines attest to an advanced society with well-developed religious, commercial, economic and administrative structures and a high level of artistic attainment. The palace, besides being the ruler's residence, would also have been the administrative headquarters of a monarch who wielded absolute power.

The palace was built of large, well-trimmed blocks of limestone (of three different kinds), mud (as a bonding agent) and sun-dried bricks. The walls were finished with lime plaster, either coloured or decorated with frescoes of scenes from nature and everyday life. Wood was used for the doors, the ceilings, the columns supporting the ceilings and the door and window jambs. The columns were wider at the top than at the base. All these materials were cut and trimmed with bronze tools, as the art of iron smelting had not yet been discovered.

Nowhere in the vicinity is there any sign of walls to protect the palace or town against enemy attack: evidently the local rulers in different parts of Crete were on peaceful terms, and moreover the existence of a road network suggests that there was regular communication and co-operation between the palaces. The possibility of attack from abroad could hardly have caused any worries, as the Minoan fleet exercised undisputed control of the seas surrounding Crete.

1

2

3

1

3

Mycenae, Tiryns: fortified palaces of 1500-1100 B.C.

Whereas the Minoans lived in unfortified towns and palaces without feeling that they were in danger, in the Peloponnese and Central Greece from about 1500 B.C. it was normal to build an acropolis, that is a hilltop citadel containing the ruler's palace, workshops, storehouses and dwelling-houses. The people that built the citadels at Mycenae and Tiryns (1) in the Peloponnese, at Gla in Boeotia and elsewhere were the Achaeans (2), who had gradually infiltrated into the Balkan peninsula from the north round about 2000 B.C. Many centuries later, one of their local kings established himself as the most powerful of their rulers: he was Agamemnon, whose palace was at Mycenae, described by Homer as "rich in gold". The first person to locate and excavate the acropolis of Mycenae, having been led there by reading Homer, was Heinrich Schliemann, who gave the name "Mycenaean" to the civilization it represented.

The most impressive feature of Mycenaean architecture is the massiveness of the acropolis walls. The Greeks of later centuries called these walls "Cyclopean" because they

believed that only giants such as the mythical Cyclopes would have been strong enough to manhandle the huge blocks of stone (3), which, with a minimum of trimming, fitted together perfectly with no mortar. The walls at Mycenae are from 6 to 10 metres thick; at Tiryns they are as much as 17.5 metres thick in some places, with tunnel-like galleries (casemates) inside them.

2

The megaron

The central nucleus of the palace crowning the hilltop was the megaron (4), which consisted of a large rectangular room with a circular hearth in the middle, a smoke-hole in the roof directly above it and four columns to support the roof. It was entered through a two-columned porch and an anteroom. The royal family's living quarters and various auxiliary buildings were laid out round the megaron.
The walls were built of stones and mud with a plaster facing on which frescoes were painted. The walls and doors were adorned with alabaster ornaments of fine workmanship, and the discovery of a bathroom shows that the Mycenaeans had a high standard of living.
Lesser mortals had their houses on the hillsides below the acropolis. Here lived the artisans, farmers and stockbreeders whose lives were spent working for the king, who supervised their work, collected and stored their produce, traded with other local rulers and was responsible for the defence of his whole realm.

The end of the prehistoric age

These fortified towns and their civilization based on a flourishing seaborne trade came to a sudden end. Round about 1100 b.c. the palaces were destroyed in a great catastrophe, probably a fresh wave of invaders, since there is widespread evidence of destruction by fire. With them, the whole structure of the Mycenaean civilization collapsed.

4

1. Workshop area

2. Bakery

3. Street of workshops

4. Bastion

5. South gate

6. North gate

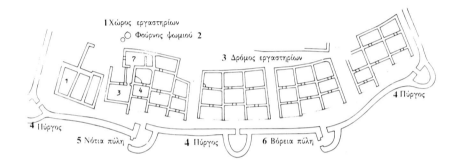

Aigina

On an abrupt headland near Aigina town, where there now stands a single ruined column from the classical Temple of Apollo, the island's Neolithic inhabitants built a village. Working first with wattle (wooden stakes interwoven with twigs and branches) attached to the natural rock, and later with stones, clay, wood and seaweed, they constructed a honeycomb of small rooms abutting on each other, enclosed within a defensive wall. In one of the rooms they had a kiln to fire their pottery. Time passed and the village fell into ruin. A second village was built on the rubble of the first, and then a third and a fourth. By this time the people had learnt to use metal and their village boasted a bronze foundry, the first known metalworking shop in Greece. The fifth village, dating from 2200-2050 B.C., consisted of houses laid out in regular, more or less rectangular blocks separated by proper streets, as shown in the plan (1). It was surrounded by a wall with several gates, reinforced with semicircular bastions. Thus by the third millennium B.C. these villages already possessed all the features that were developed later in the cities and towns of historic times.

Crete

Gournia, situated on a hilltop near the Gulf of Mirabello, is the best-preserved Minoan village. Dating from about 1500-1450 B.C., it consists of a mass of small houses packed together inside and outside the main "ring road" (3). The surviving walls are those of the ground-floor rooms, which were used for storage, while the residential quarters were on the upper floor, reached by staircases from the street. Stone blocks and the natural rock were used for the foundations, and the walls were made of bricks. Mortar was used as a wall plaster, floor paving and binding agent. The discovery of pottery, metalworking and carpentry workshops and wine and olive presses indicates that the village was an industrial centre. Other features of interest in this organized little community are the remains of a larger house in the centre, perhaps belonging to the local ruler, and of a one-room shrine.

Thera

In addition to what we can learn from excavation of the foundations, there is a fresco from Akrotiri on the island of Thera (2) that gives us some idea of what a prehistoric urban settlement actually looked like. It shows us a seaside town built on steep slopes overlooking the harbour – and we know that trade flourished in the Aegean in the seventeenth century B.C. The houses, of two or more storeys, are built of dressed stone and stout wooden beams and are painted in different colours. Some of the inhabitants are standing on the wide, flat roofs (like the roofs of most Cycladic houses nowadays) looking down at the ships sailing offshore.

2

3

Thessaly

This (1) is the floor plan of the biggest house in the Neolithic settlement of Dimini, which probably belonged to the local ruler. It is of some interest because this was the ground plan from which several architectural forms evolved later, such as the Mycenaean megaron and the Classical temple. Some idea of the appearance of the house itself can be obtained from the clay model (2) found at Kranon, the oldest of its kind in Europe (5th millennium B.C.).

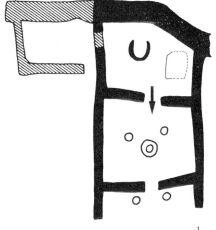

1

2

Crete

In the Iraklion Museum there is a collection of small faience plaques painted to resemble the fronts of Minoan houses. The walls appear to be built of bricks and horizontal timbers: this is very similar to the type of construction using stones, bricks and timber framing that is found in Cretan villages today and has proved highly resistant to earthquakes. A clay model (4) from Arkhanes, Crete, represents a two-storeyed house of 1600 B.C. which is roofless, perhaps because the roof was made of some other material that has perished. With its ground-floor veranda and first-floor balcony and its numerous windows, this must have been a refreshingly cool house in the Mediterranean summer.

3

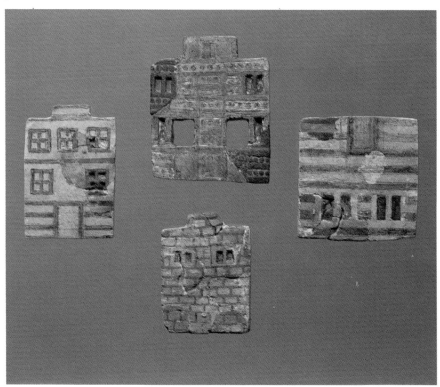

Excavations on Thera

Excavations on Thera have uncovered a large part of the prehistoric settlement. The volcanic ash that blanketed the town after the eruption of the Thera volcano in the sixteenth century B.C. has preserved in relatively good condition the two-storey and three-storey houses that would otherwise have collapsed and crumbled away. The timbers had rotted by the time the site was excavated, but their imprints were still visible on the solidified ash, and with these as a guide the archaeologists have been able to reconstruct the timbering in plaster or concrete.

4

5

From monarchy to democracy

In the communities we have been looking at so far, in Minoan Crete and Mycenaean Greece, the most important buildings were the palaces and the hilltop citadels. Both of these served the practical and religious needs of the kings, who were at once political and religious leaders.
From about 1100 B.C. onwards we see a process of gradual change in the economy, the system of government and the social structure. Community affairs, defence and administration ceased to be the responsibility of a single ruler: they were undertaken by a number of persons who were elected by all the citizens to exercise authority, either individually or as a body, within specified limits for a limited term. This new system of government, which first took shape in Athens and was subsequently adopted in some other Greek *poleis*, was called democracy.

Architecture kept in step with these social and administrative reforms to meet the changing needs of the community, and new types of building came into being to cater for the new way of life and system of government.

The *polis*

According to Aristotle (4th cent. B.C.), the location and planning of a *polis* or city had to satisfy four requirements: health, defence, suitability for political activity, beauty. About five hundred years later, in the second century A.D., the travel writer Pausanias had reservations about classifying Panopeus, a place in Phokis, as a *polis*, because it had no gymnasium, no theatre, no civic centre (agora) and no public fountains.

In an ancient Greek *polis* every citizen had a duty to know and obey the laws and to serve in the forces, as judges or jurymen and as responsible civil servants, and so they enjoyed the benefits arising from the honest administration of the community. In the Classical period the citizens of

Greek *poleis* played their part in the decision-making, funding and construction of civic amenities such as temples, theatres, stoas, gymnasia, stadia, public fountains and aqueducts. None of these were regarded as luxuries: they were simply part of the way of life.

We then have to ask ourselves by what process an ordinary village or country town evolved into a *polis* or city. Who decided on its planning, and how were the decisions arrived at? In ancient Greece a *polis* might develop in one of two ways: by the Attic (or unplanned) process or according to the Hippodamian system.

1. Agora
2. Areopagus
3. Acropolis
4. Dipylon Gate
5. Temple of Olympian Zeus

1

Attic (unplanned) urban development

Most cities grew naturally from an original nucleus of a prehistoric village or fortified hilltop settlement. When these settlements developed into cities in the Archaic period, the new buildings were erected next to or on top of the old ones, leaving the old streets, lanes and footpaths unchanged as well as the old fortification walls, which of course were essential for the community's defence. The result of this process of development was, to a planner's mind, chaos: the houses were crammed too close together and the water supply and drainage systems were inefficient.

One of the most striking examples of a city with unplanned development was Athens (1) – so much so that the ancient Greeks apparently used the term "Attic" to describe the process of haphazard, unplanned growth. Dikaiarchos, a writer of the third century B.C., was very disappointed by the appearance of the city when he visited it for the first time: he described it as "badly planned by the standards of antiquity".

The Hippodamian system

Some ancient cities – mostly overseas colonies founded by emigrant Greeks and cities that were rebuilt after being destroyed – were laid out according to a master plan from the outset. An example is Miletos in Asia Minor, which was destroyed by the Persians in 494 B.C. and then completely rebuilt according to the Hippodamian system, so called after the Milesian philosopher and town planner Hippodamos. The hub of every such city was the agora or civic centre, an open space roughly in the middle of a regular rectangular grid of houses and other buildings. Cities laid out in this way include Piraeus, Olynthos in Chalkidike and Priene in Asia Minor (2), and in the Hellenistic and Roman periods the Hippodamian system was widely adopted in all parts of the Mediterranean basin.

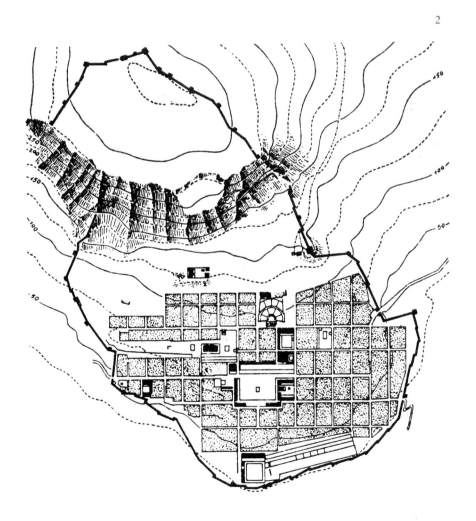

2

23

Streets and boulevards

In towns of the Archaic and Classical periods the streets were usually narrow and winding, but in the great Hellenistic cities it was a quite different story. In Alexandria there were seven parallel boulevards, the central one of which was 31 metres wide, intersected at right angles by a large number of streets. Each boulevard had a tree-lined central reservation one metre wide, dividing the road into two lanes. One lane was paved with flagstones and was for the use of horsemen; the other, surfaced with compacted earth and gravel, was for chariots and carts. Pedestrians walked in the arcades that ran along both sides of the streets and boulevards. At Ephesos the main streets, which were similarly paved with marble, were illuminated by flaming torches and automatically cleaned with water from the fountains installed at intervals along them. The road from the agora of Corinth to the port of Lechaion (1) was also paved with flagstones.

1

3

Travelling across country

Besides the city streets, there was an extensive network of roads linking the cities and small country towns. These roads had to be kept in good condition, not only for travellers on horses or donkeys but also for carts, which were used for most of the overland trade and transport. Road-building was extremely hard work, especially in rugged areas or when it was necessary to build retaining walls or make cuttings through the rock.

Bridges

Even in prehistoric times, large or small bridges were built of wood or stone to carry roads across rivers or ravines. Those that have survived attest to the ancient Greeks' skill in bridge-building. The great four-arched bridge across the Eleusinian Kephisos (the modern Sarandapotamos), fifty metres long and eight metres wide (2), was probably built in Hadrian's reign. It was discovered in 1961 when the new Athens-Corinth road was being built and is preserved in very good condition.

The Sacred Way

One of the best-known roads in antiquity was the Sacred Way which ran from the Sacred Gate in Athens to the Sanctuary of Demeter at Eleusis, a distance of twenty kilometres. It had an average width of five metres and was edged with untrimmed stones on either side. The roadway was packed with large and small stones and earth. In sandy areas a causeway of rough stones had to be built first, and in the hills the rocks had to be hacked away to make a flat surface. In several places the original roadway, rutted by cartwheels, is still to be seen. The distance from the city of Athens was marked with milestones (*horoi*) at the side of the road. The one illustrated on the facing page (4), which was found at Dhafni, bears the inscription *I ΕΞ ΑΣΤΕΩΣ*, i.e. ten [Roman miles] from the city (as a numeral, the letter I = 10).

Building regulations

In the Classical period there were laws to regulate building construction, as one would expect, and bodies corresponding to present-day planning authorities. There were also road-building contractors and architects responsible for repairs to the roads, the maintenance of public buildings and observance of the building regulations. However, it should not be supposed that they always managed to prevent violations: doorsteps and balconies were always being built out into the road, as we learn from a decree of Hippias (late 6th cent. B.C.) prohibiting such practices.

2

Orientation

Town houses in historical times varied greatly in their methods of construction and design, which depended on the location, the climate and the length of the owner's purse. Usually they were small, built of inexpensive materials, and with little outside ornamentation in comparison with contemporary public buildings and temples.

From what ancient writers had to say on the subject, it appears that the orientation of their houses was what people were most concerned about. Xenophon, in his *Oikonomikos* (a treatise on household and estate management), recommends that houses should face south so that the rooms would get the sun in winter and be cool in summer. The Roman architect Vitruvius, in his *De Architectura*, makes the following comments: "Streets and houses should be laid out in such a way as to be protected from the strong winds that blow in every region. Cold winds are unpleasant, hot winds enervating, moist winds unhealthy. Whatever happens, people building houses should avoid the mistakes made at Mytilene, where the south winds make people ill and the north-west winds make them cough. When the wind is in the north the cough goes away, but what good is that when it's too cold to poke your nose out of the door?"

General layout

The ancient Greeks liked their homes to be guarded by Hestia, the goddess of the hearth and household, and protected both from the winds and from the eyes of passers-by. The hub of the house was an inner courtyard (or sometimes two, but not more), either opening straight off the street or further inside, with the rooms arranged round it. Air and light for the rooms came from the courtyard, as there were seldom windows opening on to the street.

In the yard there was always an altar dedicated to Zeus Herkeios, the "protector of the walled courtyard", which was used for family acts of worship. On one side of the yard the upper floor, if there was one, was supported on columns or piers made of wood or stone, forming a covered colonnade at ground-floor level. Water was supplied by a well or cistern, usually in the courtyard. The way into the house was through a porch and a large door leading into

1

2

the high-walled courtyard (1, 2, 3).
The head of the household had his
own reception room, the *andron*,
which was always on the ground
floor and was the biggest and best
room in the house. There he would
entertain his male friends at *symposia*
(drinking-parties) in the evening.
Nearby there was a separate living-
room, the *gynaikonites*, for the
women, children and female slaves,
often with a built-in hearth in the
middle and with portable braziers for
additional warmth in the winter. In
two-storey houses the *gynaikonites*
was usually on the upper floor, with
the bedrooms.

Downstairs there were a number of
domestic offices opening off the yard:
kitchens, bathrooms, storerooms for
various purposes (according to
Xenophon, "Wheat goes in the driest
storeroom, wine in the coolest,
pottery and works of art in the best-
lit") and a stable, or often a shop or
workshop with a street door, which
the house-owner might use himself or
let out to a tradesman.

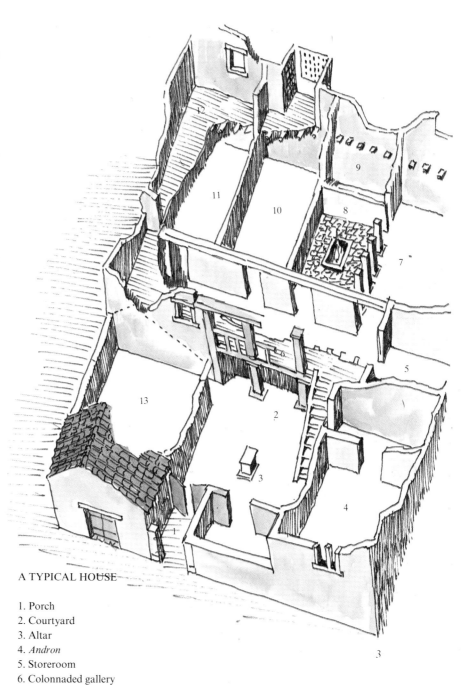

A TYPICAL HOUSE

1. Porch
2. Courtyard
3. Altar
4. *Andron*
5. Storeroom
6. Colonnaded gallery
7. Kitchen
8. Hearth
9. Bathroom
10, 11. Living-rooms
12. *Gynaikonites*
13. Shop, workshop or storeroom

In Athens

Ancient Greek writers tell us a good deal about Athenian houses, and the literary evidence has been supplemented by archaeological finds: for example, a fairly large house has been excavated between the Pnyx and the Areopagus, in what was a residential area (1). Windows opening on to the street were rare: where they existed, they were display windows for shops or workshops.

At Vari

Houses in the country were different from town houses. At Vari, in Attica, excavators have uncovered the walls of a farmhouse that seems to have been very similar to a farmhouse of today (2). The tower at one corner of the courtyard was presumably used as a watchtower and for storage. Near the house there would have been beehives (made of clay) and a walled or fenced enclosure for the farm animals.

On Delos

The streets in the town of Delos were narrow and winding, as they still are in the Cyclades. Doors and windows were smaller because of the hot summer sun and the strong winds that blow all the year round. The roofs were not tiled but flat, to collect every drop of rainwater for storage in the cisterns (3).

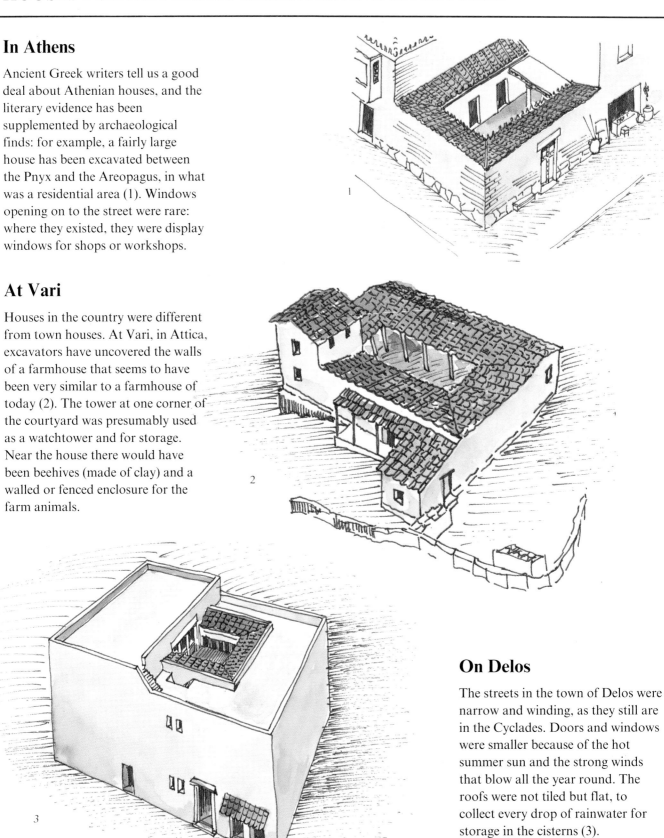

At Olynthos

At Olynthos, in the Chalkidike peninsula, there are the remains of a Classical town in a better state of preservation than any other in Greece. Like Piraeus (4), it was laid out on the Hippodamian grid plan. The grid consists of identical rectangular housing blocks with two rows of five houses in each block, but within the uniformity of the overall dimensions there is considerable variety in the floor plans of individual houses.

At Pella

At Pella, capital of the kingdom of Macedonia, the design of the houses was different. The wealthy had bigger homes (5) with marble colonnades round the courtyards and floors decorated with mosaics. This type of house came to prevail all round the eastern Mediterranean in the Hellenistic period.

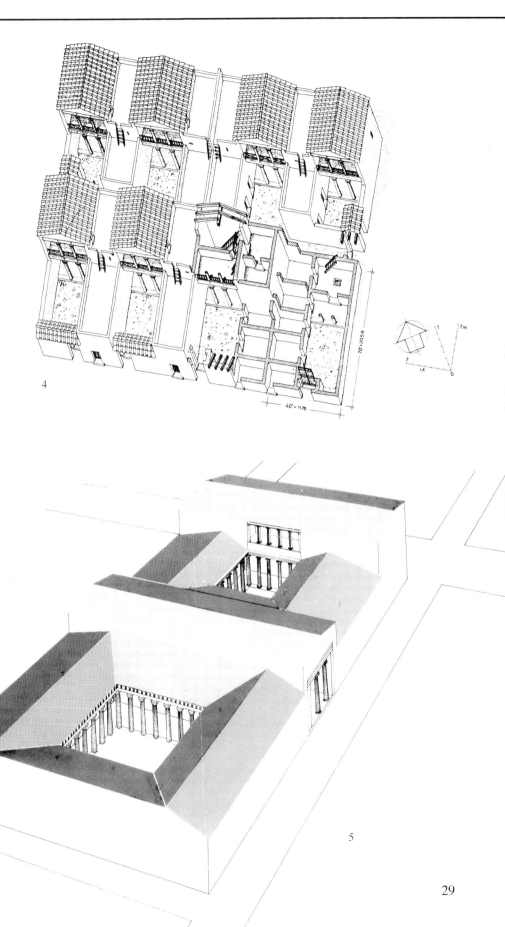

4

5

ARCHITECTURAL FEATURES AND ORNAMENTATION

Whereas most houses were fairly similar in their external appearance, their interiors varied considerably in the materials used, quality of construction and taste.

Floors

In ancient Greece the floors of private houses, and of many large buildings too, were made of compacted earth. Excavations on Delos have brought to light a number of marble cylinders which were apparently used as rollers, to keep the floor as flat as possible so as to prevent dust from gathering.

Mosaic floors

Many town houses had mosaic floors, especially in the courtyards and certain rooms such as the *andron*. As early as the end of the fifth century B.C. mosaics were being made with white and naturally coloured pebbles from river beds and beaches, which were laid in a bed of mortar to form simple or more elaborate designs. Pebble mosaics were also used to make figural compositions, as in some houses at Pella.

Later mosaics were made of tesserae (square-cut pieces of natural stone or coloured glass) instead of pebbles. The new technique made it possible to produce magnificent mosaic floors in a wide variety of colours, like the ones on Delos (1, 2) and at Dion, Macedonia, illustrating scenes from mythology or everyday life. Mosaic floors, whether made of pebbles or tesserae, were usually watered regularly to keep them wet, so as to bring out the colours and also to cool the room or courtyard.

Paved and wooden floors

The floors of large public buildings and temples were paved with large marble flagstones, and in the Roman period it became common for ordinary houses to be floored with smaller earthenware tiles. Upper floors were usually wooden, consisting of floorboards resting on wooden joists which fitted into rectangular sockets in the walls. A few houses with their upper storeys have survived on Delos and at Ammotopos, Epiros, as well as defensive towers in city walls and elsewhere, many of them up to four storeys high.

1

Roofs

The roofs of ancient Greek houses were like the tiled roofs one still sees today and were usually simple pitched roofs (i.e. with two surfaces sloping downwards from a central ridge). A supporting truss of timbers was covered with planks, mud and straw, and finally the tiles.

Tiles

Ancient tiles were usually made of clay, although in some special cases (e.g. the Parthenon) they were of marble. They were of two types, the Laconian and the Corinthian (3, 4), and were known either as "stretchers" or as "capping-tiles" according to the way they were laid. From the lowest stretcher in each row the water ran out into a continuous horizontal gutter along the edge of the roof known as the sima (5), which was usually decorated with painted motifs such as palmettes, meanders and scrolling stems, with lion's-head spouts.

Antefixes

The lowest capping-tiles were adorned at their outer ends with floral antefixes, forming a row along the edge of the roof. These, with the designs painted on the sima, gave a decorative finish to the building.

2

3

4

5

Doors and windows

The doors of private houses, and of larger buildings too, were made of wood, sometimes faced with a metal overlay on the outside. They usually opened outwards, which could be dangerous for passers-by, so it was normal practice to knock on the door before going out, rather than before entering! Doors provided a measure of protection not only for the occupants of a house, many of whom were tenants, but also for the house-owners, who were permitted by law to remove the doors if a tenant was consistently in arrears with his rent. No ancient wooden doors have survived, but a good deal is known about their appearance from vase-paintings (1) and also from the doors of Macedonian tombs, which were marble replicas of wooden doors. The rows of round metal studs at the top, middle and bottom of a door were the heads of the nails that held the planks together. Besides serving this functional purpose they also had a decorative effect, which is often imitated to this day (2).

Bolts, handles, door-knockers

Nailed on to the door were metal handles with palmette-shaped ends and metal door-knockers which were often made in decorative shapes. Also made of metal (bronze or iron) were the bolts which secured the door to the lintel and doorsill, and the locks and keys. Ancient keys were much heavier than those in use today, but the basic mechanism of the locks was very much the same.

2

1

The doorsill

The one part of the doorway that survives in very good condition, at nearly all excavated sites, is the sill. As a rule it consists of a single large flat block of stone, worn down by the tread of feet. The sockets and grooves cut in the sill make it possible to work out exactly how the door opened and closed.

Here (3) we have a plan view of the doorsill of a house excavated at Olynthos and a reconstruction drawing of the front door. The shallow rectangular cavities in the sill (shaded in the drawing) were for the wooden jambs, while the deeper round or rectangular sockets next to them held the vertical pivots on which the door turned. With the exception of a few heavy doors in large temples, ancient doors were not attached to the jambs with hinges in the modern way: they turned on the metal-encased pivots projecting at the top and bottom of their inside edge, which rotated in sockets (also lined with metal) in the sill and lintel, rather like the door of a modern refrigerator. In the middle of the sill there were smaller sockets for the bolts. The transverse grooves allowed water to drain out of the courtyard into the road.

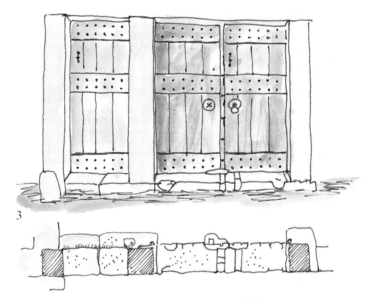

3

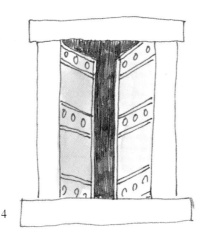

4

Windows

The windows of houses in ancient Greece were neither as numerous nor as large as they are nowadays. They were constructed in the same way as the doors (4). As a rule, the only ones opening on to the street were shop windows. This one on Delos (5), measuring 1×2 m., has marks on the jambs indicating that there was an iron grille to prevent thieves from breaking in and stealing the goods on display.

It has been suggested, though without firm evidence, that window apertures were closed with thin sheets of vellum which were stretched taut and oiled or greased to make them translucent. Glass window panes were unknown before the Roman period.

5

THE AGORA

The central feature of every ancient Greek city, and the one which best sums up its way of life, was the agora or civic centre. Even in the earliest settlements it is clear that the inhabitants felt the need for a main square, an open space where they met to deliberate on issues of war or peace and to hold athletic contests or religious ceremonies.

The word *agora*, which was already in use in Homer's time, is derived from the verb *ageiro*, meaning "gather" or "assemble". It was in the agora, for example, that the Phaeacians gathered to meet Odysseus and to compete in discus-throwing contests. In historical times the agora was usually in the centre of the city or near the harbour and was the hub of the citizens' political, religious and business life. The buildings erected in and around the agora reflected its threefold character: administrative, religious and commercial.

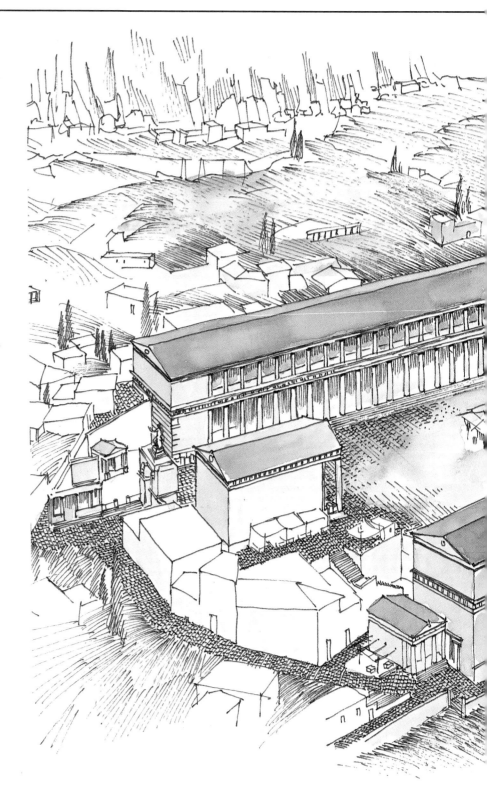

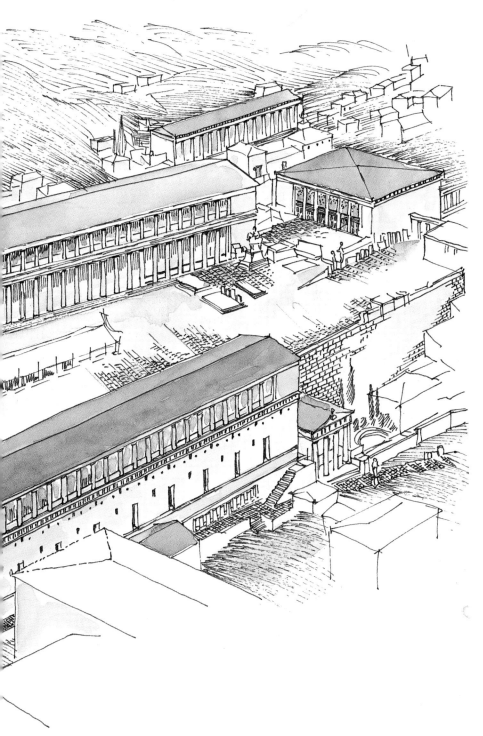

At Assos

At Assos, a Greek city situated on a steeply-sloping hillside near Troy, it was necessary to build a broad artificial terrace supported by a massive retaining wall in order to have a level space for the agora, which was traversed by the main street (1).

The imposing buildings round the sides of the agora, constructed in different periods, attest to its multiple character. The temple stands at one end, and facing it at the other end is the Bouleuterion (Council House). The stelai visible outside the Bouleuterion were inscribed with the texts of laws and decrees, which it was the duty of every citizen to be familiar with. The two long colonnaded buildings are stoas. The two-storey north stoa contained shops, and the open-fronted gallery was used by itinerant vendors and also for public meetings in bad weather. The south stoa was three storeys high, with a public bathhouse occupying the whole of one of the upper floors. Trade was carried on not only in the north stoa but also in small shops near the temple and at stalls set up under awnings in the square. The atmosphere would have been that of a street market, and we can imagine the agora full of people all day long, some of them bargaining with the stallholders while others stood about discussing matters of moment or, if they had nothing better to do, strolling up and down and gossiping.

1

Stoas were long, narrow structures with a wall along the back and a colonnade supporting the roof along the front. The stoa, which might be a building on its own or an arcade forming part of a bigger building, was a purely Greek architectural form. Stoas were to be found everywhere – attached to private houses and gymnasia, in agoras and in sanctuaries. The reason for their ubiquitous presence is that they were ideally suited to the Greek climate and way of life: in them the townspeople, who usually spent most of the day out of the house, could find shelter from the burning sun in summer and from sudden rainstorms or icy winds in winter.

The interior of a stoa was so simple that it could be adapted for many different uses, by night as well as by day: the oldest known stoa, one with wooden columns at the Sanctuary of Hera on Samos, was used as a hostelry for visiting pilgrims.

For public administration

One of the oldest stoas in the Athens Agora was known as the Royal Stoa because the King Archon, one of the city's nine chief magistrates, had his offices there. Its function, therefore, was purely administrative. Solon's laws were inscribed on the walls of the building and on triangular stone tablets attached to the façade.

For philosophical discussions

Next to the Royal Stoa stood the Stoa of Zeus Eleutherios, a religious building consecrated to the worship of Zeus as the god of liberty and deliverance. For many Athenians this was a favourite place for strolling about and meeting their friends. As Plato informs us in his dialogues, philosophers were in the habit of discussing the problems of life while sitting on the stone benches or walking up and down in the stoa.

2

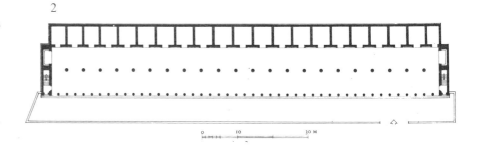

Diogenes the Cynic, who had no fixed abode and generally slept out in public places, used to say that the Athenians had built the Stoa of Zeus Eleutherios so that he could have a roof over his head.

For Stoics

The Stoa Poikile or Painted Stoa took its name from the beautiful pictures that covered its walls. Painted by great fifth-century artists such as Polygnotos, Mikon and Panainos (brother of the sculptor Pheidias), they depicted scenes from the Amazonomachy, the fall of Troy and the battles of Marathon and Oinoe. This stoa, too, was a haunt of philosophers. It was here that Zeno of Kition gave lessons in the fourth and third centuries B.C.: he was the founder of what became known as the Stoic school of philosophy, taking its name from this building. Zeno, incidentally, was the first person to advocate a world civilization, a community of nations with no frontiers and no wars.

Shopping malls

On the east side of the Athens Agora a two-storeyed ancient stoa has been completely rebuilt (1, 2). It was originally erected in the middle of the second century B.C. by Attalos II, king of Pergamon in Asia Minor, partly in token of his gratitude to the city where he had studied and partly to win honour and glory for himself. The stoa, which was named after him, soon became a favourite meeting-place for the Athenians. It functioned as a shopping mall, with forty-two shops on the two floors

selling mainly luxury goods: jewellery, expensive fabrics, ceramics, cosmetics, perfumes and herbs, toys and so on. The shopkeepers rented the premises from the state, paying a high price for the privilege. During the Panathenaia festival the upper colonnade provided an excellent grandstand for watching the great religious procession which started from the Dipylon Gate and passed right in front of the stoa on its way across the Agora and up to the Acropolis.

Reconstruction

The Stoa of Attalos was reconstructed in 1953-1956, after years of study of the building stone

found on the site and painstaking calculation of all the technical details. The materials used were exactly the same as in the original building – Pentelic marble, porous limestone from Attica and tiles made of Attic clay – with one exception: the rafters, instead of being made of wood, are of reinforced concrete painted to look like wood (3). Replicas had to be made of four different types of capitals for the 134 columns (45 in the outer colonnade and 22 in the inner colonnade on each floor). The rooms that used to be shops now house the Agora Museum, offices, storerooms and all the documentary records of the excavations and the reconstruction project.

3

The stoas could not cater for all the administrative and social needs of a *polis* with a democratic constitution. The assembly of all the citizens and the smaller executive and administrative bodies had to have other meeting-places, either indoors or out of doors, specially adapted to their requirements.

"Who wishes to speak?"

The first essential in a democratic society is that every citizen should be able to express his opinions in a responsible manner. A meeting-place was therefore needed, with enough room for all the citizens (5,000-10,000 at the very least in Athens), so that all could take part in the deliberations on issues that concerned them and arrive at a collective decision. The place chosen for this official assembly in Athens was a small hill called the Pnyx, situated in a populous residential area with a panoramic view over the Agora, the Acropolis and the Areopagus and right down to the sea. A large level terrace was made in the natural slope of the hill (1), and there the *Ekklesia* (Assembly of the People) met thirty or forty times a year. Every Athenian male over the age of twenty who had finished his military service had the right to vote in the Ekklesia, and also to speak on any item on the agenda: to do so, he would put a wreath on his head and mount the steps to the rostrum, which was carved out of the rock. Every person present at the meeting received a small attendance allowance of 2 obols, to ensure that impecunious workers who were losing a day's wages by attending would not suffer financially.

The topics debated at meetings of the Ekklesia covered every department of the city's life, including religious, political, legislative, judicial and economic issues. Any citizen could propose a motion for debate and submit it in advance to the Boule (see p. 40), which drew up the agenda. A motion passed by a majority vote was enacted into law as a *psephisma* (decree), and the text was written out on a sheet of papyrus which was kept in the public archives (in the Metroön). If the matter was one that had to be made known to all the citizens, the text of the decree was carved on a stone stele, starting with the words "It has been resolved by the Boule and the people": many such stelai have survived. All the great Athenian statesmen addressed the people from the rostrum of the Pnyx: here Themistokles stood to urge his fellow-citizens to fortify their city without delay after it had been sacked by the Persians; here Perikles, against the opposition of the rival party, urged the Athenians to spend the surplus tribute from their allies in the Confederacy on the construction of the Parthenon.

1

2

The changing shape of the Pnyx

The landscaping and layout of the Pnyx went through several phases. At the end of the sixth century B.C., when Kleisthenes established a democratic constitution, the citizens gathered on the hillside facing the Areopagus and the speaker stood at the bottom of the slope. In the fifth century the orientation was reversed, with the people facing south (towards the sea) and the speaker facing the Agora, and at the same time the assembly ground was enlarged by partial excavation of the hillside and the construction of a banked-up terrace. What we see today is the third phase, dating from the middle of the fourth century B.C.

The terrace was further enlarged and a massive semicircular retaining wall was built of huge rectangular blocks of stone quarried on the Pnyx itself, creating a more or less semicircular floor.

In the Roman period the Ekklesia met in the Theatre of Dionysos, which was better suited to the purpose because it had a seating capacity of about 15,000.

The most important administrative buildings in ancient Athens, namely the Bouleuterion, the Tholos and the Metroön, stood in a group on the west side of the Agora.

The Boule of 500

The *Boule* (Council or Senate) was a body of citizens who had advisory and judicial powers and also drafted legislation. It had five hundred members, fifty from each of the ten "tribes" into which Kleisthenes divided the population of Attica at the end of the sixth century B.C. Any male citizen over thirty who had done his military service was eligible for membership. Every citizen had the right to question the honesty and moral integrity of any member of the Boule, and also to scrutinize the draft texts of laws proposed by the Boule to the Ekklesia. The Boule met every day, except on public holidays, and from the time of Perikles each member was paid an allowance equal to an artisan's daily wage for every session he attended.

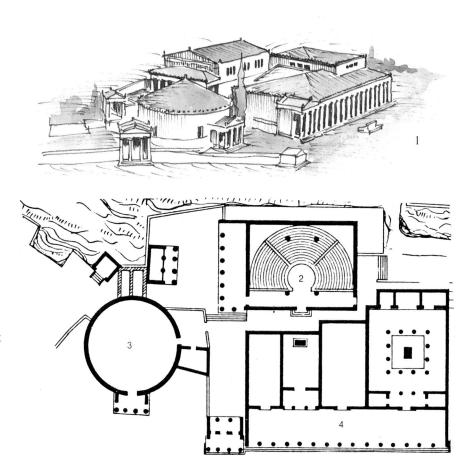

The Bouleuterion

The Bouleuterion was the meeting-house of the Boule. The one in Athens (2) was built at the end of the sixth century B.C., when Kleisthenes established the Boule. It is 22.5 m. long by 17.5 m. wide, and the hollow curve of the natural rock in the interior indicates that the seating area was arranged like an ancient theatre, perhaps with wooden benches for the councillors (who must have been rather cramped when all five hundred of them were there). The speaker's rostrum was probably also made of wood.

The Prytaneis

The ten "tribal" groups of fifty Councillors took it in turns to wield supreme executive power for one-tenth of the year (35 or 36 days) each. The fifty men in office at any given time were the *Prytaneis*, who were responsible for convening the Boule and Ekklesia and drawing up the agenda for their meetings. Every day one of their number was drawn by lot to be their Chairman (*Epistates*), who for that day held the Great Seal and the keys of the temples where the public treasury was kept. The Chairman of the Prytaneis was the highest officer of the Athenian Republic: in fact he was a sort of President, but only for twenty-four hours.

The Tholos or Prytaneion

The Prytaneis held their meetings in the Tholos. This was a plain rotunda, 18 metres in diameter, with a conical roof of lozenge-shaped tiles supported by six interior columns (3). There was an altar in the centre. The building had just one door, and presumably there were windows to admit light. It was destroyed over and over again, and rebuilt each time. In the Roman period a four-columned porch was added on to the entrance.

The Tholos was also used for the safe keeping of the city's official standard weights and measures, which excavators have found on the site. These were receptacles for liquids and dry goods and were used by the *metronomoi*, official inspectors whose job it was to prevent dishonest merchants from cheating the consumers.

The Metroön

The word "Metroön" is derived from the Greek for "mother" and was used to denote a temple of Rhea, the mother of the gods. The Metroön in Athens (4) was divided into four sections. One was like a small temple, with the altar of Rhea in front of it, outside the portico. The two rooms on either side were used for the storage of the archives. The fourth section, which was two-storeyed and had a central courtyard, resembles an ancient Athenian house in its ground plan: it may have been the official residence of the city registrar.

In Athens, the Metroön combined the function of shrine with that of public records office. All the state archives and other official documents were kept there, such as the minutes of meetings of the Boule, which were written on papyrus or parchment. The secretary of the Boule was responsible for keeping the minutes and having its decrees transcribed on to stone stelai or white wooden boards, which were then set out on the front of the Monument of the Eponymous Heroes to be read by the citizens (5).

Register of citizens

Among the other documents kept in the Metroön was the register of Athenian citizens. This explains why the word *mitroön* is used in Modern Greek even today to mean a register.

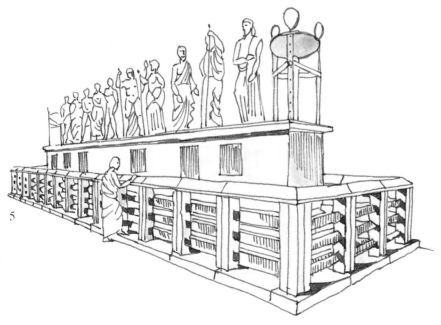

5

Just as there were no professional politicians in ancient Greece, nor were there any professional judges. It was considered to be the duty of every Athenian citizen to offer the state his skills and expertise in an administrative or judicial capacity, to the best of his ability. Democracy and justice in Athens relied on amateurs, who held most of the public offices in rotation and were required to be sufficiently familiar with the legislation in force to be able to administer justice on the basis of the law and their own consciences. The Heliaia and the Areopagus were the two main tribunals dealing with civil and criminal cases respectively, and the Boule and Ekklesia also had the authority to hear certain cases.

The Heliaia

The Heliaia, with 6,000 members, was the largest judicial body. Sometimes it met in plenary session, and sometimes in smaller divisions of 501, 1,001, 1,501 or 2,001 members. Those who were called on to perform this public service were paid a sum approximately equal to a labourer's daily wage for each day's attendance. It is not known where the various tribunals of the Heliaia met: in early times, an open space on the south side of the Agora may have been used for this purpose. A building excavated beneath the Stoa of Attalos was almost certainly a law court, as an urn containing bronze voting discs for the use of jurors (1) was found in it, but it must have been used by a smaller tribunal.

The Areopagus

The Areopagus (in Greek, *Areios Pagos*) is a rocky outcrop between the Acropolis and the Pnyx. The ancient Athenians derived its name from Ares, the god of war, but most probably it was connected with an earlier sanctuary of the Furies (*Arai*). The name was also applied to the Council of the Areopagus, a body of Athenian citizens derived from the council of nobles that existed under the kings of the Mycenaean period and later probably held its meetings on the level ground near the rock, to the north-west of the entrance to the Acropolis.

In the Classical period the Areopagus tried murder cases, which were heard out of doors so that the judges should not be sullied by being under the same roof as the murderer. It also had jurisdiction in cases involving religious offences, which were heard in the Royal Stoa in the Agora (2). One of its duties was to pass judgment on foreign religions, so it was probably before the Council of the Areopagus that St. Paul expounded the doctrines of Christianity when he came to Athens in A.D. 52.

1

2

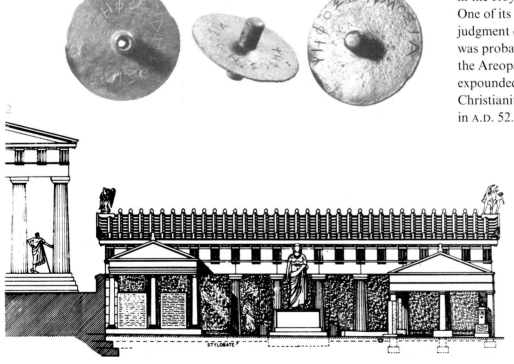

The Athens prison

Another essential public building was the prison, which in ancient Greece was generally used only for the short-term detention of convicts awaiting sentence of death, the most usual penalties being the forfeiture of property to the state and sentences of exile. In Athens the prison is thought to have been somewhere near the Agora. A likely candidate is a large (40×17 m.) limestone building erected in the mid fifth century b.c., the foundations of which have been found nearby (3).

A narrow corridor with rooms opening off it on either side leads from the gate to a big courtyard at the back. Next to the gate was a separate four-roomed block set at an oblique angle. This curious complex has been variously interpreted as a law court, an inn or public offices. But it could have been a prison, in which case the rooms would be cells, the courtyard an exercise yard or a compound for mass arrests, and the gate block the warders' living quarters.

The discovery in a pit of thirteen small vases of the third century b.c. (4), of the kind used for medicines, suggests that the building may have been a public dispensary. However, those who maintain that it was a prison believe that the vases were storage jars for hemlock, which was used for the execution of condemned prisoners. Another object found in the excavation was a Hellenistic statuette of Socrates: this may have been a memorial offering from the Athenians, who very soon realized what a mistake they had made in executing one of the greatest thinkers of the ancient world.

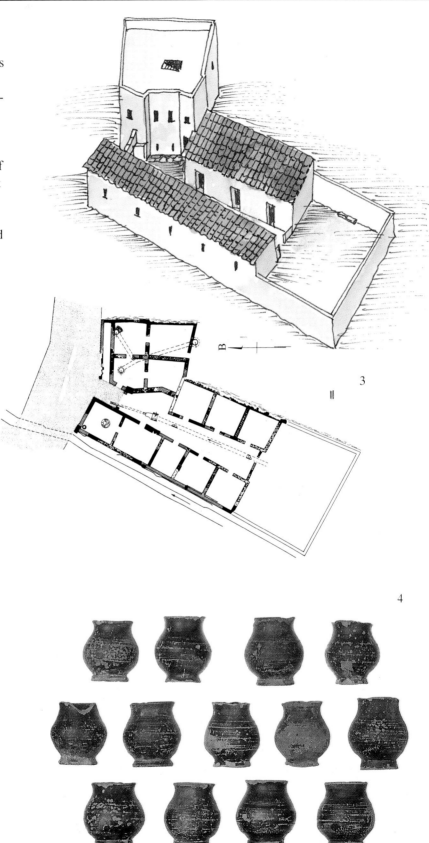

3

4

The Great Dionysia

In the early spring, at any time from mid-March onwards, most Greek cities celebrated the Great Dionysia festival in honour of Dionysos, the god of vegetation and the harvest. The proceedings started with celebrations and sacrifices, and the streets were full of revellers singing, dancing and parading in torchlight processions until late into the night. This was followed by some days of theatrical performances. From the time of Peisistratos (6th cent. B.C.), when the Dionysia was officially established in Athens as a state festival, drama developed continuously and steady progress was made with theatre design.

Greek theatres

The original meaning of the word *theatron* is "a place for viewing", and the orchestra (the circular floor between the front seats and the stage area) was "a place for dancing". (from *orcheisthai*, to dance). Dionysiac festivals may have originated in the country, where farmers hoped to propitiate Dionysos and so ensure a good harvest by performing songs and dances in his honour. In time these performances, still religious in character, spread to the cities. In Athens they were put on in the Agora, with a semicircular grandstand of wooden benches for spectators. Eventually, owing to the growth of audiences and the risk of the stands' collapsing under the weight, it seemed more sensible to create a more permanent viewing-place where the spectators would be safer, and the obvious solution was to use a natural hollow in a hillside,

1

where everybody would be able to see and hear the performers.

In Athens, the Theatre of Dionysos was built on the south slope of the Acropolis (1). The hillside was excavated and banked up where necessary to create a regular hollow semicircle with rows of wooden seats. In the fourth century B.C. the wooden seats were replaced with semicircular rows of stone seating (much of it marble), which was solid and more comfortable for the spectators. The seating area (*cavea*) was divided by horizontal pathways (*diazomata*) and vertical flights of steps into wedge-shaped blocks (*kerkides*). Facing the spectators at the back of the orchestra was the *skene*, a single-

storey or two-storey scene-building (2). The semicircular open-air theatre was an original architectural invention of the ancient Greeks, as were the stoa and the Greek temple. Theatres were built all over the Greek world around the shores of the Mediterranean. In Greece itself there were about seventy, in sanctuaries of Dionysos and Asklepios and also in cities. The earliest date from the sixth and fifth centuries, but the finest examples, such as the one at Aspendos in Asia Minor (3) and the famous one designed by Polykleitos at Epidauros, were built in the fourth century. The biggest theatre in Greece was the one at Megalopolis, which had a capacity of over 21,000.

Acoustics

The theatre architect's main concern was to ensure good acoustics. The sounds of the actors' and singers' voices should not be magnified too much or reverberate for so long that they re-echo, nor should they die away. By a process of observation and mathematical calculation, the ancient Greek architects came up with a design that allowed the very faintest sounds to be heard with absolute clarity by everyone in the audience. Sometimes large earthenware jars were placed at strategic points in the cavea to improve the acoustics.

2

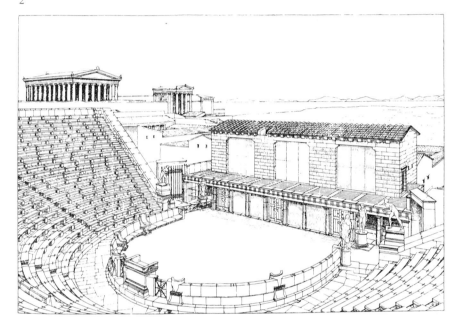

3

1

Besides the theatre, the ancient Greeks also enjoyed singing, instrumental music and poetry readings, all of which formed part of their education. However, Greek theatres were not suitable for musical competitions, for which a smaller auditorium was needed, and so the odeion came into existence. It was similar to a theatre in shape and construction, but was smaller and had a roof. Odeia were used mainly for concerts but sometimes also as courtrooms or for public philosophical debates.

Odeion of Perikles

The oldest odeion in Athens was the one built by Perikles for the musical competitions of the Panathenaia festival. Situated on the south slope of the Acropolis (1), it was, with the nearby Theatre of Dionysos and the later Odeion of Herodes Atticus, part of the world's first centre for the performing arts.

The building was almost square, with a roof said to have been modelled on that of the tent on Mt. Aigaleos from which Xerxes watched the battle of Salamis. The roof was supported by row upon row of wooden posts which may have been made from the masts of Persian ships captured in the battle. The performers stood in the centre, with the audience sitting all round.

Odeion of Herodes Atticus

Two more odeia were built in Athens in the Roman period: that of Agrippa in the Agora and another one, presented to the city by the enormously wealthy rhetorician Herodes Atticus in honour of his wife Ania Regilla, at the foot of the south-west corner of the Acropolis (2). The Odeion of Herodes Atticus was built of Pentelic marble and its roof, made of cedar wood with no interior columns or posts to support it, was particularly admired by everybody who saw it.

Theatres and city planning

The position of the theatre in a city, or outside it, varied from place to place. The chosen site was normally a hillside needing a minimum of excavation and embankment, where the theatre would fit in aesthetically with the other buildings round about. Often it was on the slope of an acropolis or near the agora, as theatres were used for other public gatherings as well as drama performances. Sometimes theatres were built on flat ground: one such was at Mantineia in the Peloponnese, where a massive retaining wall had to be built at great cost to support the cavea.

3

2

Choregic monuments

The costs of putting on a theatrical production were defrayed by wealthy private citizens, who undertook to act as sponsors (*choregoi* or *choragoi*) and were jointly responsible with the playwright for all the production arrangements. The choregos paid the wages of the actors, musicians and chorus and covered their living expenses and the cost of their costumes from the start of rehearsals until the performance was over. In compensation for this drain on their purses the choregoi won official recognition from the state as well as high social status.

If the production won a prize, the choregos received a large bronze or gilt tripod, This he would set up on a small monument (a "choregic" or "choragic" monument) near the theatre or somewhere else in the city, with an inscription giving the name of the choregos, the "tribe" to which he belonged, the names of the Eponymous Archon for the year and of the prize-winning playwright, and the title of the play.

The Monument of Lysikrates in Athens (3) is one of the best-preserved choregic monuments. It served as a pedestal for the tripod won by a certain Lysikrates, who sponsored a chorus of boys of the Akamantis tribe in the archonship of Euainetos, i.e. 334 B.C. This graceful little structure, a miniature tholos, has Corinthian columns surmounted by a frieze depicting the abduction of Dionysos, the god of the theatre, by Tyrrhenian pirates while on a voyage to Delphi. The tripod itself has not survived.

Books

The first texts to be made into books in Greece were the works of Homer, which were written on sheets of animal skin or panels of wood for use by minstrels. Books came into wider use in the sixth century with the development of literary and philosophical works, poetry and plays, which were not so easy to transmit orally.

Towards the end of the fifth century, Egyptian paper made from the leaves of the papyrus plant was introduced into Athens from Byblos in Phoenicia, and when papyrus started to be grown in Greece the use of paper spread more rapidly. Another major development was the introduction of parchment, a material made from animal skins, which originated at Pergamon in the second century B.C. With parchment it was much easier to write (and to erase writing) on both sides.

The first books either took the form of long rolls of writing material or were made of folded sheets sewn together, and were usually kept in bookcases. Naturally they were extremely expensive at first: only the wealthiest rulers, such as Peisistratos of Athens and Polykrates of Samos, could afford to have private libraries, though later Euripides and Aristotle both had libraries of their own. By about the fourth century the Greeks had started establishing large collections of books for public use, but it was not until the Hellenistic period that special buildings were erected for the purpose. It was then that scholars became interested in preserving and studying the "ancient wisdom" with academic rigour and full awareness of its value.

The two most famous libraries in the ancient world were at Alexandria and Pergamon, the very places where papyrus and parchment were first used as writing materials. In Athens two large libraries, those of Hadrian and Pantainos, were established in the Roman period.

The Library of Alexandria

Nothing whatever remains of the library at Alexandria, but we know from ancient sources that it was part of the Mouseion, a large establishment of higher education so called because it was devoted to the veneration of the nine Muses, the patronesses of the arts, literature, philosophy and the sciences. The Mouseion could accommodate 14,000 students, researchers, scholars, artists and other intellectuals.

The library was founded by the Ptolemies, the Hellenistic kings of Egypt, who spent enormous sums of money on its enlargement and enrichment. Ptolemy III, for example, put down a deposit of fifteen talents – a huge sum – to borrow the official manuscripts of the works of the great tragedians from Athens, and then refused to return them as he was more interested in keeping the manuscripts than in getting his money back. He is also said to have given orders that any manuscripts on board ships arriving in Alexandria harbour were to be seized, and copies given to the ships' masters in exchange. By practices of this kind the library grew apace, so that by the second century B.C. it had some 700,000 books. Alexandria was also renowned for its literary scholars. It was there that the first commentaries on the works of ancient Greek authors were written, and there too that a team of seventy scholars translated the Old Testament into Greek, the lingua franca of the civilized world.

Pergamon

The ruins of a few rooms are all that remain today of the library at Pergamon in Asia Minor. In each room there was a balustrade one metre high running parallel to the wall at a distance from it of 45 cm., to prevent library users from handling the books. The books were kept in shelves attached to the walls, as we can tell from the sockets in the masonry. These rooms had double walls to insulate the books from damp. To visualize the library in its heyday, we have to imagine it full of wooden tables and chairs. Another feature of the Pergamon library was a large lecture room.

Hadrian's Library

Hadrian's Library, one of the two in Athens of which the ruins have been found, was a huge building, 122×82 m. overall, with an inner peristyle courtyard (1) planted with trees and shrubs. In the middle of the courtyard was a long pool (58×13 m.) to provide a refreshing and soothing atmosphere for the scholars and students holding earnest discussions in the cloisters. The books were kept in the middle room on the east side. The discovery of a speaker's platform and 15-18 rows of stone lecterns in each of the two flanking rooms suggests that they were used for lectures.

Library of Pantainos

The Library of Pantainos was situated on the east side of the Agora, next to the Stoa of Attalos. According to an inscription carved on the lintel of the main door, the funds for the construction of the building, the books and the decoration of the library were donated by one Pantainos, who dedicated the library to Athena and the Emperor Trajan. This means that it must have been built *circa* A.D. 100.

Library hours

Another inscription (2) informs us, as it informed the library users in antiquity, that books could not be borrowed and that the library was open "from the first to the sixth hour" (i.e. from sunrise to sunset).

1

2

Gymnastics and society

In ancient Greece, physical exercise for the young went hand in hand with the cultivation of their minds and was placed on an equal footing. It was a regular part of their daily lives (1) and was organized by the state. Sporting competition and festivals of games were purely Greek concepts, although other peoples had competitive events of a less highly-developed kind in prehistoric times. The Panhellenic festivals of games held in religious sanctuaries, in honour of the gods worshipped there, evolved into highly prestigious occasions attracting entrants from all over the known world. In this way physical prowess and superior fitness, originally regarded as military virtues, came to be a medium for reconciliation and peacemaking, because the beginning of an Olympiad was the signal for the cessation of all hostilities.

Gymnasia and palaistrai

Gymnasia and palaistrai were the buildings used for daily exercise and also for special training for the competitive sporting events held in stadia and hippodromes.

In the sixth and fifth centuries a gymnasium presumably consisted of an expanse of level ground with a few outbuildings (such as changing-rooms) for the use of the athletes. From the fourth century, however, it gradually developed an architectural form of its own, with buildings and facilities of many different kinds: stoas, baths, changing-rooms, storerooms, rest rooms and so on, and even classrooms and lecture halls. So the gymnasium became a centre of intellectual as well as physical education where lessons were open to any citizen wanting to improve his mind, and not only the young. By the end of the ancient era the word "gymnasium" had come to

mean a school in the broadest sense of the word, as it does to this day in Greece and some other countries such as Germany.

Gymnasia were usually built outside the cities, where there was plenty of open space, but there were also quite a number inside the city boundaries. The three largest and oldest gymnasia of ancient Athens were the *Akademia* (in the sacred grove of that name where Plato established his school of philosophy, the "Academy"), the *Lykeion* or *Lyceum* (in what is now the National Gardens, between Syntagma Square and the Panathenaic Stadium) and the *Kynosarges* (near the Church of St. Panteleimon by the River Ilissos). Others, such as that of Diogenes and that of Ptolemy, were built later within the city walls. There were also gymnasia and palaistrai in sanctuaries great and small, where athletes could train for the games.

1

GYMNASIUM AT DELPHI
1. Entrance
2. Xystos*
3. Paradromis*
4. Palaistra*
5. Peristyle
6. Offices
7. Bath area
8. Round pool
9. Hot baths

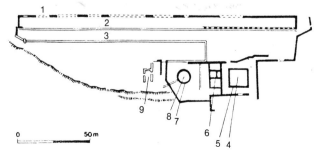

2

The facilities

The usual form of a gymnasium was a square or rectangular building, always with an inner courtyard surrounded by colonnaded galleries and rooms which athletes and others connected with the gymnasium could use for practice and other purposes. There had to be sandpits for the wrestlers and long-jumpers, running-tracks of the right length, and special facilities for discus-throwing and other events. The auxiliary offices had to include changing-rooms, a storeroom for olive oil, an *aleipterion* (a room where the athletes rubbed their bodies with oil after exercise) and baths. Another essential was a covered area where practising could be done for all events, including running races, in the event of bad weather – an indoor gymnasium, in other words. There was also an office for the *gymnasiarchos*, an official appointed by the state with responsibility for the education of the young, as well as rooms or facilities of some sort for schoolteachers and lecturers.

The gymnasium at Delphi (1, 2) was on two levels. On the upper level were two running-tracks each about 180 metres long (i.e. one *stadion*, the length of the track in an ancient Greek stadium) for training for foot-races. One, called the *xystos*, was a covered colonnade for use in bad weather. Next to it was the open-air *paradromis* for use when the weather was fine. On the lower level was the *palaistra* (a building used as a school for wrestling and other sports), consisting of a central courtyard with a colonnade on all four sides and rooms at the back. West of the palaistra there is a round pool big enough to swim in (about 10 m. in diameter and 1.80 m. deep), which was filled with water from the Castalian Spring. Behind the pool there were large washbasins with a constant supply of fresh water from spouts in the wall above them.

Stadia

Stadia were the places used for "gymnic contests", in other words track events. The *stadion* was originally a unit of length (in English, a stade) equal to 600 feet (*podes*), varying from 177.50 to 192.28 metres in different parts of Greece, which was the basic unit of distance for foot-races. Hence the word came to be used for the building where such races were run. Typically, the site chosen for a stadium was a flat stretch of land with sloping ground on either side, which needed the minimum of earth-moving to make a flat running-track for the athletes and banks of seating for the spectators on three sides (2).

One of the oldest stadia in the ancient world was the one at Olympia, which was also the most prestigious even though it never had stone seats for the spectators. Other important stadia with complicated mechanisms for the starting gate were at Isthmia, Delphi and Nemea (2).
In Athens, the Panathenaic Stadium (1), used for the games that formed part of the Panathenaia festival in Athena's honour, was situated in a fold of Ardettos Hill on the banks of the Ilissos, outside the city walls. The site was first adapted as a sports ground by Lykourgos in about 330 B.C., but it was not until the Roman period that Herodes Atticus, that great benefactor of Athens, paid for the construction of an all-marble

stadium for the Panathenaia of A.D. 144. Its thorough restoration in the late nineteenth century for the first Olympic Games of the modern era (1896) makes it possible for visitors today to admire an ancient stadium in its pristine glory.
The Panathenaic Stadium is shaped like an elongated horseshoe. The overall dimensions of the running-track area are 204×33.50 m. There are fifty tiers of marble seats divided into blocks by seven staircases at the curved end (the *sphendone*) and eleven staircases along each side, giving it a capacity of about fifty thousand.

Hippodromes

A hippodrome was a larger version of a stadium used for horse-races and chariot-races (4). The general layout of the track and the spectators' stands was the same as in a stadium, but here there was always a *sphendone* to allow the horses and chariots to take the turn at speed. The two straight sections of the track, each two stades in length, were separated by a stone wall or wooden fence, the *embolon*. The jockeys and charioteers raced over several laps, each lap being four stades long. Practically nothing now remains of any Classical hippodrome, but ancient writers have left descriptions: Pausanias, for example, describes the hippodrome at Olympia (3) and gives a detailed description of the mechanism of the starting-gate. The signal for the start was given by simultaneously lowering a bronze dolphin to the ground and hoisting a

2

1. Altar with eagle
2. Starting stalls
3. Bronze dolphin
4. Winning-post
5. Stewards' box
6. Embankments for spectators

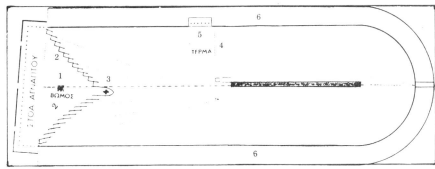

bronze eagle (which was on the altar) into the air, whereupon the horses or chariots were released in quick succession from their stalls in such a way that they all started in a straight line abreast.

It was mainly at the great religious festivals, when sporting and musical competitions were held, that the need arose for what we would now call tourist facilities. As far as food was concerned, there were always enough bread, olives, fruit and nuts to go round. Accommodation for tourists *en masse* was not considered necessary: most visitors slept under the stars, in tents or in the stoas.

Hotels for VIPs

For official guests and wealthy visitors special accommodation was available in hotels (*katagogia*), which provided all the amenities such people would expect. Hotels existed at all sanctuaries, the most luxurious ones being the Leonidaion at Olympia and the *katagogion* at Epidauros (1).

The Leonidaion was so called after the benefactor who paid for its construction, whose name has been found in an inscription on the architrave: *Leonidas of Naxos, son of Leotas, made [this] and dedicated it to Olympian Zeus.* It was an almost square building with an exterior colonnade of 138 Ionic columns. An interior peristyle courtyard was laid out with gardens and ponds.

The *katagogion* at Epidauros, built at the end of the fourth century B.C., had 160 rooms on two floors laid out round four peristyle courtyards.

The word *katagogion* is still in use in Greek, but only in the sense of an insalubrious "dive", because of the number of inns frequented by disreputable characters.

Leschai (Clubhouses)

Another type of building intended for the use of tourists was the *lesche*, which provided no overnight accommodation but only facilities for social gatherings. The best-known *lesche* was that of the Knidians at Delphi, a single large room with wall-paintings by Polygnotos, where visitors to the sanctuary could rest and pass the time in conversation.

A similar purpose was served by the so-called *Pinakotheke* or "Art Gallery" (2), one of the rooms of the Propylaia on the Acropolis in Athens, which was equipped with couches and was so called because it had paintings on the walls by the great fifth-century painters Mikon and Polygnotos. It was actually not an art gallery as such but a place where rich visitors to the Acropolis could sit down and rest after toiling up the steep steps.

1

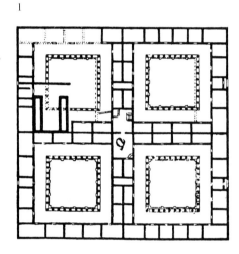

2

Baths

Bathrooms existed from prehistoric times in the royal palaces of Crete and Mycenae. Homer makes a point of mentioning the baths his heroes took to refresh themselves after battles, shipwrecks and sundry other adventures. The bathrooms in Cretan palaces were very luxurious (3), but in houses of the Classical period they were much simpler. Earthenware bathtubs found at Olynthos are very similar to those of our own time, but with no plughole.

Public toilets

Public toilets were provided by the state and were very necessary in ancient Greek cities, not only for visitors but for local residents too, since no toilet facilities existed in most houses.

In the Roman Agora in Athens there was one such public convenience that could seat sixty-four persons. It was an elegant building consisting of a large, almost square room, roofed but open for ventilation in the centre, where the roof was supported by four columns. The seats, ranged along the wall on all four sides, were made of marble carefully rounded and smoothed for comfort, with a constant stream of clean water flowing underneath (4). In this companionable atmosphere people could carry on discussing the burning issues of the day without interruption.

3

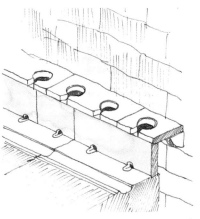

4

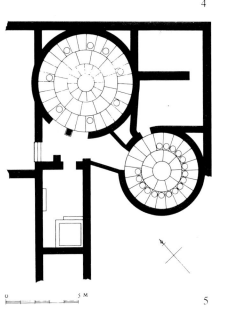

5

Public baths

Most people performed their ablutions at public bath-houses or public fountains.

The well-preserved remains of a typical early bath-house are to be seen at Oiniadai in Akarnania, Western Greece (5). It contains a small rectangular room with a square water tank used for cold baths, and two circular rooms as typically found in bath-houses. In the larger of the two circular rooms there were eight round tubs spaced round the centre, and in the middle there was probably a copper boiler to provide warm water. The smaller circular room contained seventeen tubs with a boiler in the middle for hot water. This arrangement allowed users to have a bath at any of three different temperatures or even all three in succession, which they often did, savouring the different kinds of pleasure to be had from each.

The Roman period was the great heyday of public baths in antiquity. Huge bath-houses were built, with large rooms decorated with mosaics, statues and marble floors and walls. For hot baths the Romans used *hypocausts*, which were basement rooms in which great fires were kept burning to heat the water tanks in the rooms above.

Bath-houses were usually located outside the cities so that travellers could wash and refresh themselves before entering the city gates. There were separate facilities for men and women.

1

The Minoan palace aqueduct

Water supply and sewage systems already existed in Greece in the Minoan period: the architect of the palace at Knossos knew a good deal about cisterns, wells and the principles of hydraulics, as we can tell from the engineering of an aqueduct that brought water from a spring 10 km. away. The construction of the water pipe, its size, the thickness of the pipe wall, the method used to connect the sections and the degree of incline are all carefully worked out to ensure a regular flow of water. There is also a complex drainage system to carry away rainwater and waste water.

A famous cistern

On the acropolis of Mycenae there is a subterranean cistern eighteen metres below ground. Known as the Spring of Perseus, it was fed by an earthenware pipe from a source 360 metres away. It is reached by a rock-cut staircase of eighty-three steps, of which the last twenty were covered when the cistern was full of water. This was a notable feat of engineering for its time.

The tunnel of Eupalinos

Technologically advanced water supply and drainage systems were installed in many Greek cities in historical times, when good rulers generally made a point of linking their names with some major public works project of this kind.
On Samos, a famous aqueduct built in the sixth century B.C., when the island was ruled by Polykrates, supplied water to the ancient city (on the site of the modern village of Pythagorio) for a thousand years. Herodotos tells us that it was engineered by Eupalinos, an architect from Megara. The most remarkable part of the aqueduct is the tunnel, 1,036 metres long, that was cut through a hill (2). Eupalinos's calculations were so accurate that the tunnellers worked from both ends simultaneously and were almost exactly on target when they met in the middle. The water ran along a channel cut in the tunnel floor, with a constant gradient, and the whole aqueduct worked simply by gravity.

Hadrian's aqueduct

The aqueduct built by the Emperor Hadrian in Athens worked on the principle of interconnecting compartments. It brought water from Mt. Parnes and Mt. Pentelikon to a big reservoir (still in use) at the foot of Lykabettos, above Kolonaki Square. In places the conduit was tunnelled through the rock (sometimes as much as 45 m. below the surface); elsewhere it was carried high above the ground on arches (1). Part of one of these arched sections is still standing in the Nea Ionia area, north-east of central Athens.

2

The Enneakrounos Fountain

In the sixth century B.C. the Athenian ruler Peisistratos built a fountain-house in the Athenian Agora, known as the Enneakrounos, which was fed from the Kallirrhoe Spring near the River Ilissos. It was famed both for its architectural elegance and for its cool, refreshing water, which was used at wedding ceremonies for the bride's ritual ablutions.

Opinion differs among archaeologists as to whether the name Enneakrounos was applied specifically to this fountain with its nine lion's-head spouts (*ennea*, nine; *krounos*, spring), so often depicted in vase-paintings (3), or to a whole system of conduits bringing water to nine different fountains in the city (*krene*, fountain or spring).

Be that as it may, the Enneakrounos was not the only public fountain in the Agora: there were three others besides, from which some of the water was channelled off to make a network of running streams with basins and troughs at intervals for the benefit of animals and plants as well as human beings. There were also a number of fountain-houses elsewhere in the city, mostly near the gates (like the one at the Dipylon Gate) for travellers to refresh themselves after their journey. The illustration below shows a Hellenistic fountain-house of strikingly attractive simplicity at Priene in Asia Minor (4).

3

4

Wells

The rest of a city's water supply consisted of wells and cisterns. In the Athens Agora there were about 400 wells built at different times over a period of a thousand years, as we can tell not only from the remains of the wells themselves but also from the broken pots found in them by the excavators.

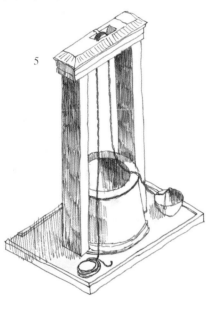

5

Cisterns

In places where water is in short supply, such as the islands of the Cyclades, there were cisterns and reservoirs everywhere. On the island of Delos most of the houses had cisterns faced with waterproof cement underneath their courtyards (6), and there was also a huge cistern (15.50×6.30 m.) to collect rainwater from the theatre. This last is of some architectural interest for the arches supporting the roof.

At Kameiros, on Rhodes, there is a cistern of the Archaic period notable for the pozzolana-based cement that was used to make it waterproof. Similar cisterns have been found in many other places, including the Sanctuary of Hera at Perachora, near Corinth (7).

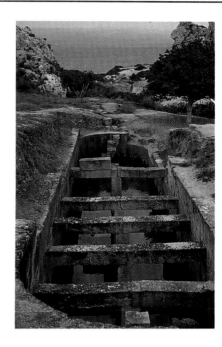

7

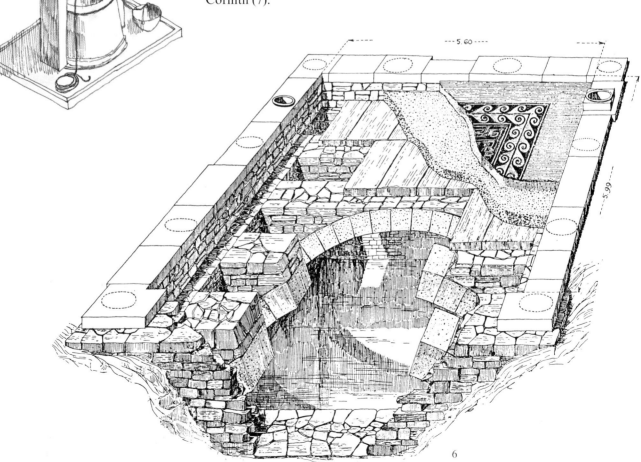

6

8

Water pipes

The pipes that brought water from springs or streams to the cisterns and public fountains were generally made of clay and had the maker's name incised on them (8).

Lead water pipes are found less often, because the harmful effects of lead on human health were already known. Vitruvius is forthright in his condemnation of them and gives a full medical explanation of the hazards they present: "Their harmful effect is to be seen in artisans working in lead foundries, whose bodies are exposed to the gases. Little by little, their limbs are deprived of all the vigour of the blood. That is why drinking water should on no account be carried in lead pipes."

Drains

Waste water and rainwater were carried away by a network of drains. The drainage system in the Athens Agora, which survives almost in its entirety, emptied into the River Eridanos. Its main storm drain, built of masonry, was big enough to cope with the most torrential downpour and still functions perfectly today (9).

Upkeep of the water mains

Besides the technical skills required for its construction, the water supply system also needed maintenance. In Athens, the Superintendents of Fountains (as Aristotle calls them) were elected for a four-year term. Their job was a very responsible one and for that reason they were elected, whereas many other administrative posts were assigned by lot.

9

1

Harbours

Great care was taken over the construction of safe harbours, especially in the great commercial centres whose economic power was based mainly on maritime trade. Massive piers and breakwaters were built to protect ships from rough seas, and they were often fortified with walls and towers. Harbour mouths were usually just wide enough for one ship, to make it easier to defend them and, when danger threatened, to close them with a heavy chain (1).

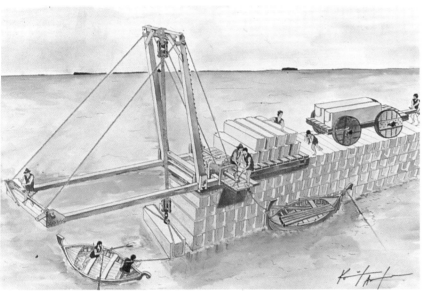

2

A good idea of how the piers were built can be obtained from the reconstruction of the methods used at the port of Amathous in Cyprus (2). The huge blocks of stone were moved and lowered into place by a stoutly-constructed travelling crane which moved along the pier, resting on the last section to be built.

Shipsheds

Among the other important
dockyard facilities were the
shipsheds, solidly-constructed
buildings where warships were laid
up in winter, when all naval
operations were suspended (3). They
were 30-35 m. long and about 6.50
m. wide, with a saddle roof
supported by unfluted columns. Each
shipshed was large enough to store
one or two triremes, which were
hauled up on to wooden slipways.
There were many such shipsheds or
boathouses in Piraeus (in the main
harbour and the Zea basin), and also
at Sounion and other ports.

The Skeuotheke

Another essential building in any
port was the *skeuotheke* or rigging
store (4), where warships' masts and
spars, sails, anchors, ropes, chains
and similar items were kept.
The best-known one was Philon's
Skeuotheke in Piraeus, which takes
its name from the architect who
designed it and supervised its
construction. Its foundations were
discovered a few years ago near Zea
harbour, but the shape, size and
general appearance of the building
had long been known from an
inscription recording the contract for
its construction, which gives all the
architectural and structural
specifications (5).

3

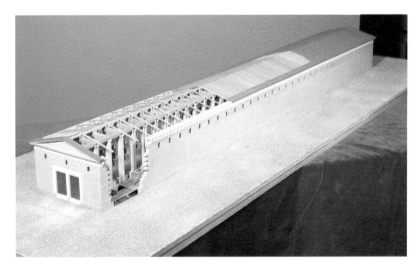

4

5

The Clock of Andronikos Kyrrhestes ("Tower of the Winds")

"Some people maintain that there are only four winds, but careful observers tell us there are eight. The most important of those observers is Andronikos, who, to prove his point, built an octagonal marble tower in Athens. On each face of the octagon he put a relief depicting the wind that blows from that direction (1) and at the top there was a conical roof of marble. At its apex he set a bronze Triton with a staff in his hand, which rotated with the wind and showed the precise direction in which it was blowing."

So Vitruvius describes the little tower built by the astronomer Andronikos of Kyrrhos, which was erected in the first century A.D. in the Roman Agora in Athens and is still standing. Apparently it housed the mechanism of a klepsydra or water-clock, and on the south face there was a sundial so that people walking through the crowded market-place could see the time from far off.

1

The Pharos at Alexandria

Lighthouses were numerous in antiquity, but there was one that so far surpassed all others in size and magnificence that it was counted as one of the seven wonders of the ancient world. This was the Pharos at Alexandria (2), the city in Egypt founded by Alexander the Great which was the most important port in the Mediterranean for over a thousand years.

The lighthouse at Alexandria was built by the Ptolemies, the dynasty that ruled Egypt after Alexander's death. It took its name from the offshore islet of Pharos on which it stood, and such was its fame that the word *pharos* was used to mean a lighthouse for ever after. At night its beam of light was visible from a distance of 300 *stadia* (about 55 km.), and in daytime its smoke could be seen from much further away.

The Pharos was a tower about 120 metres high, with a spiral ramp inside for mules to carry firewood up from ground level to the beacon-fire at the top. The outside walls were of white stone adorned with splendid marble and bronze ornaments, such as the statues of Tritons at the top of the tall base section, which were greatly admired. Crowning the whole edifice was a colossal statue of Poseidon holding a trident in one hand and pointing down at the sea with the other. A dedicatory inscription lower down gave the name of the architect, who had already won a wide reputation with his earlier buildings:

"Sostratos, son of Dexiphanes, dedicates this to the gods who look after travellers."

The Pharos needed constant maintenance and was still being repaired well into the Middle Ages. It is said to have been finally destroyed by a severe earthquake early in the fourteenth century. Its appearance is known to us from contemporary coins (3) and numerous descriptions in travellers' writings.

In 1995 a number of large stone building blocks from the base section of the Pharos and some of the statues were found in the sea just off the islet.

3

2

3

Fortifications

Building fortification walls was one of the biggest drains on the budget of every ancient city, but defences were needed to protect the inhabitants' lives and property, and they had to be formidable enough to daunt any potential attacker and command the respect of visitors to the city.

The walls were usually built after the city, following the outline of the built-up area. Special care was taken over the fortification of the acropolis – the hilltop citadel which was the last line of defence when the city was attacked – and of the port, which was vital to the city's survival.

Construction

The height and construction of the walls varied from city to city and from one period to another. In Athens, the Classical city wall was as much as 10 metres high in some places on the west side. Its lower courses were built of stone, its upper courses of sun-dried bricks which were faced with mortar and capped with tiles to prevent them from being washed away by rain.

Gates and towers

The city wall of Athens was reinforced at intervals with towers and gatehouses guarding the roads that led out to the towns and villages of Attica and the rest of Greece. Thirteen of the city gates have been located so far, as well as two more opening on to the corridor between the Long Walls connecting Athens with Piraeus.

The Dipylon was the main gate into the city. It was protected by four towers overlooking a courtyard enclosed on three sides, where attackers would be hemmed in by the defenders in the event of a sudden assault on the gate (1). Not far to the north-east was the Eriai Gate, smaller than the Dipylon and simpler in its construction. Immediately to the south of the Dipylon was the Sacred Gate (2), so called because it was through this that worshippers set out along the Sacred Way to Eleusis to attend the Eleusinian Mysteries. Smaller towns were also walled. One good example is Aigosthena, on the Attic coast of the Gulf of Corinth, where there are sections of wall still standing to a height of about 5 metres and gatehouses and square towers to a height of 13 metres, all excellently constructed. They are made of neatly-dressed blocks of hard limestone, which is plentiful thereabouts. Equally impressive is the fortress of Eleutherai (3) in north-western Attica on the frontier with Boeotia, near the Kaza gorge.

THE GATES OF ATHENS

Dipylon (or Thriasian) Gate
Eriai Gate
Acharnian Gate
N.E. Gate
Diochares Gate
Hippades Gate
Diomeian Gate
Itonian Gate
Halade (Sea) Gate
South Gate
"Dipylon above the Gates"
Melitides Gate
Demian Gate
Peiraic Gate
Sacred Gate

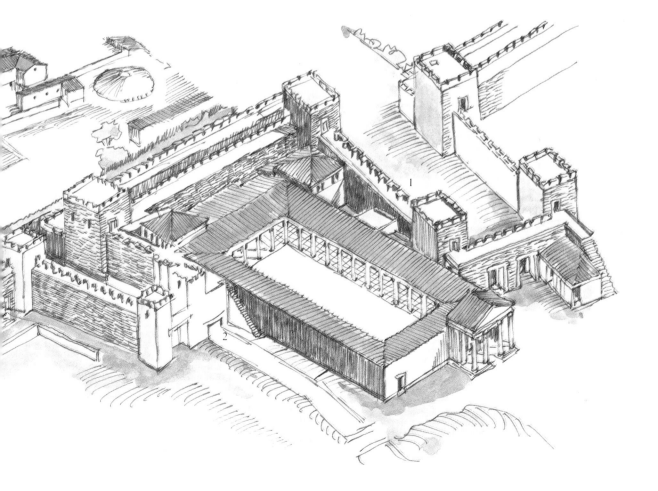

The history of a city's walls reflects the city's military history. Athens is a typical case in point.

The Mycenaean Wall

The oldest wall in Athens of which any traces remain is one built of Cyclopean masonry, like those of Mycenae and Tiryns, which was constructed round the edge of the Acropolis at the end of the Mycenaean period (1240-1220 B.C.) to protect the king's palace and his subjects' houses, which were clustered together on the hilltop. Sections of that wall, 5-6 metres thick, survive to the south of the Propylaia and in the bastion that served as a platform for the Temple of Athena Nike.

The Pelasgian Wall

At about the same time, or shortly after, a complex system of fortifications and retaining walls was built to guard the vulnerable western approach to the Acropolis and a number of springs and caves at the foot of the rock, which were important to its defence. In the Classical period this was called the Pelargian or Pelasgian Wall, perhaps because it was associated with the pre-Hellenic Pelasgian people, or sometimes the Enneapylon ("Nine-gate"), perhaps because one had to pass through a series of gates to reach the top.

The Themistoklean Wall

The first large-scale fortification wall in Athens was built in 479/8 B.C., immediately after the Persian Wars, on the initiative of Themistokles, who misled the Spartans about his

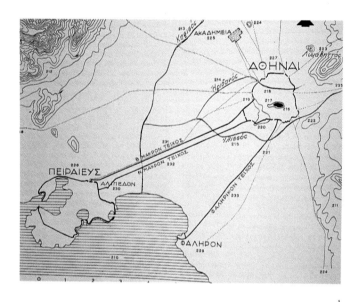

intentions by means of a cunning ruse and constructed the city's defences in a very short space of time. Thucydides gives an excellent description of the work on the project and explains that it was completed so rapidly because architectural members and sculptures from old buildings and even stones from old tombs were used for the lower courses of the walls. The upper courses were built of bricks. The wall was roughly circular in plan and enclosed all the built-up areas of the city as well as a good many open spaces (1).

Themistokles also persuaded the Athenians to fortify Piraeus at the same time. The security of the port was obviously vital to Athens as a rising maritime power, and by this time Piraeus had clearly outstripped Phaleron as the city's main harbour.

The Long Walls

It was usual in antiquity for a city situated some distance from the sea to have walls connecting it with its port, to provide safe communication between the two. In the case of Athens and Piraeus, they were known as the Long Walls (1). The North Long Wall and the Phaleric Wall were built by Kimon in 459 B.C. and in 447 Perikles added the South Long Wall, thus creating a fortified corridor seven kilometres long and 180 metres wide. This was where the inhabitants of the surrounding countryside took refuge a few years later, when the Spartan army was pillaging Attica during the Peloponnesian War.

The walls were demolished by Lysander in 404 B.C., after the defeat of Athens in the Peloponnesian War. A few years later, in 394/3, when the city had recovered her power under Konon, all the walls were rebuilt exactly where they had stood before, except for the Phaleric Wall, as the Phaleron roadstead was no longer used as a naval port. Konon's Wall lasted until 86 B.C., when the Roman general Sulla sacked the city after a bitterly-fought siege and razed the walls to humiliate the Athenians and preventing them from rebuilding their strength.

The moat

In 338 B.C. the Athenians decided to strengthen their defences in order to resist the expansionary designs of Philip of Macedon. An outer wall, the *proteichisma*, only about 5 metres high, was built about 9-10 metres in front of the Classical city wall, and that in turn was protected by a moat 11 metres wide and 4 metres deep, to be filled with water in the event of an attack on the city. These gave Athens a triple line of defence against her enemies.

The "Valerian Wall"

In the middle of the third century A.D. the Roman Emperor Valerian refortified Athens in the face of the threat from the marauding tribes of Herulians and Goths. The old walls were rebuilt and another was built further east to enclose the new part of the city ("Hadrian's city", as it was called in honour of the emperor who did so much to beautify Athens) that had grown up in the meantime. However, the new walls failed in their purpose, for in A.D. 267 Athens was overrun and sacked yet again.

The Late Roman Wall

After the Herulian raid the Athenians themselves built a far less ambitious wall as their last line of defence, using material from demolished buildings. It enclosed only one-tenth of the city, including the Acropolis and the Roman Agora, and it lasted until the Turkish period.

2

Respect and honour for the dead is one of the oldest precepts of human conduct in every culture. In ancient Greece, after the body had been prepared for burial, it was interred in a tomb hewn out of the rock or built of masonry. Sometimes it was considered necessary to erect a memorial worthy of the deceased on top of the tomb, not only to preserve his or her memory but also, indirectly, to enhance the status of the surviving members of the family. Kings and members of the ruling class were commemorated with splendid memorials that rivalled the very temples of the gods in magnificence.

1

The "Treasury of Atreus"

Imposing monuments to the dead had been built even in prehistoric times. The power of the Mycenaean kings is reflected not only in the ruins of their palaces and citadels but also in the famous "beehive" tombs, more properly known as tholos tombs. The grandest of them all is the so-called "Treasury of Atreus" outside the acropolis walls at Mycenae (1), built to accommodate the body of a dead king and the precious offerings that were buried with him for his use in the next world. The tomb was invisible from the outside because the "beehive" chamber (*tholos*) was completely covered by a mound of earth. It was approached by a long corridor (*dromos*) cut horizontally into the mound, with side walls of dressed blocks of breccia. The walls of the burial chamber consist of regular courses of stone blocks corbelled to form a pointed vault. Special care was taken over the doorway of the chamber, which was faced with green marble adorned with spirals. The lintel is of astonishing size: it is a single block of stone measuring 8×5×1.20 m. and weighing approximately 120 tons, which covers the doorway and takes the weight of the section of vault directly above it (2). We do not know how it was manoeuvred into position: the only plausible hypothesis is that it was hauled on wooden rollers up a sloping ramp of sandbags.

2

3

Burial mounds

The Mycenaean period in mainland Greece was followed by the Geometric period (10th-8th cent. B.C.), when burial mounds were the rule. These were conical mounds of earth covering one or more burials, crowned with amphoras, kraters or plain funerary stelai.

In the Archaic period (7th-6th cent. B.C.) the most splendid tombs were built for members of the well-born families of Attica and wealthy landowners in the Mesogaia plain east of Athens. They were surmounted by kouroi or korai, or by stelai adorned with sphinxes and palmettes.

In the fifth and fourth centuries, tombstones often took the form of relief stelai like that of Hegeso (3) in the Kerameikos cemetery.

Cemeteries

From the sixth century B.C. it was the custom to have properly planned cemeteries outside the walled cities or out in the country, with the graves laid out on either side of a road. Sometimes there were also a few isolated burial monuments (heroa or mausolea) inside the city walls.

The main cemetery in Athens was the Kerameikos, just outside the walls to the north-west of the city near the gates and roads leading to Piraeus, Eleusis and the rest of western Attica. Along the road leading to the Academy from the Dipylon, the principal entrance to the city, was the *Demosion Sema*, the state cemetery where, in the Classical period, prominent public figures and soldiers who had died for their country were given a state burial.

Burial enclosures

The commonest kind of funerary structure in the Classical period was the burial plot, a rectangular or circular compound with a dressed stone wall enclosing a number of graves, usually of a single family (4). Memorials of various kinds were ranged along the top of the front wall: stelai carved with floral ornaments and the names of the persons buried there, funerary reliefs and marble funerary vases (loutrophoroi and lekythoi).

4

Macedonian tombs

Another type of tomb, known as Macedonian, was used chiefly in Macedonia, Thrace and Thessaly from the fourth century B.C. It consisted of a barrel-vaulted underground chamber with a façade resembling the front of a temple, with a false porch of engaged semi-columns, an imposing doorway and Ionic or Doric entablature and pediment. These tombs were buried beneath a mound of earth that hid for ever the whole monumental edifice with all its magnificent interior and exterior ornamentation and priceless contents (the burial chamber was furnished with painted marble couches and thrones, and here too the body was interred with precious grave goods to take into the next world).

One of the best-preserved Macedonian tombs is at Lefkadia near Naoussa: it has a façade combining different architectural orders, with marvellous paintings still in a good state of preservation (5). The oldest, and archaeologically the most important, was discovered at Vergina, on the site of ancient Aigai (6). On the evidence of the exceptional splendour and outstanding quality of the grave goods found in it, as well as other indications, this has been convincingly identified as a king's tomb, probably that of Philip II of Macedon, Alexander the Great's father, who was buried there in 336 B.C.

5

6

70

The Mausoleum at Halikarnassos

One type of funerary monument of particular architectural interest was developed in Asia Minor in the fourth century B.C. as an elaborate memorial to departed kings and princes. The most magnificent example of the type was the Mausoleum at Halikarnassos (7), which was so famous that it was considered one of the seven wonders of the ancient world and its name has come to be generally used of any large and stately tomb. Construction work on the Mausoleum was started in 353 B.C. by Mausolus, satrap of Karia, and completed not long afterwards by his widow Artemisia. Its architects were Pytheos and Satyros, who wrote a book about their achievement.

Little now remains of the Mausoleum, as it was demolished in the Middle Ages so that its stones could be used in the construction of a new citadel. However, both Vitruvius and Pliny the Elder have left descriptions of it which, with the help of many surviving sculptural ornaments, have led to several conjectural reconstructions of its appearance.

Evidently the building stood on a high rectangular platform and was surrounded by a peristyle of 36 columns. Above the Ionic entablature was a pyramidal stepped roof of 24 courses crowned by a marble four-horse chariot and statues of Mausolus and Artemisia, rising to a height of over 40 m. (131 ft.). The whole building was covered with statues and reliefs by four famous Greek sculptors: Skopas, Timotheos, Bryaxes and Leochares. Some of the sculptured frieze slabs, depicting scenes from the Amazonomachy and the Centauromachy, have survived and are now in the British Museum.

7

Early cults

In the older religions of Minoan Crete and Mycenaean Greece temple buildings as such probably did exist, judging by the evidence of a somewhat later Cretan clay model of what appears to be a temple with a goddess inside and worshippers(?) on the roof (1). Religious rites were usually performed in the palace by the king, who was also the high priest – the god's vicar on earth. However, ordinary people also performed rites in places where some physical feature or natural occurrence gave them a visible sign of numinous power and a divine presence. Mountain-tops, certain caves and groves and fissures where steam emanated from the

1

ground were some of these sacred places where divinities were worshipped.

The Olympian religion

By the end of three centuries after the collapse of the Mycenaean civilization a new culture had taken its place, with different views on such matters as religion and architecture. The new religion was a fusion of the old cults with new deities and new rites brought by the last of the Hellenic tribes, the Dorians, who arrived in Greece about 1100 B.C. Since human beings feel a need for order and a stratified hierarchy, the ancient Greeks envisaged all these gods, demigods, heroes and personified natural forces as members of an extended family and wove innumerable myths round them, giving them human characteristics and setting them in situations drawn from everyday human life.

Some of the old places of worship remained in use and many new ones were created, both in the cities and in the country. All these holy sites were respected by everybody and were looked after with pious attention. Some of them – especially those dedicated to gods with oracular or healing powers, such as Delphi (2) – were treated with special veneration and developed into Panhellenic cult centres.

Politics and the priesthood

Some sanctuaries, trading on the oracular powers attributed to their gods, the priests' skill at interpreting oracles and the large amounts of money to be made out of them, acquired a great deal of political as well as religious influence, so much so that they controlled much political decision-making even at the level of

interstate relations. The Amphictyonies, religious organizations formed by the cities nearest to a sanctuary to supervise its affairs and promote its development, were so powerful that they altered the course of Greek history. Politicians often donated large sums of their own money to erect new buildings in religious sanctuaries. The aristocratic Alkmeonid family in Athens, for example, paid for the completion of the Temple of Apollo at Delphi in order to win favour with the priests so that oracles would be interpreted in their favour.

Famous festivals

The most famous Panhellenic
sanctuaries were Olympia, Nemea,
Isthmia, Epidauros, Eleusis, Delphi,
Delos (in the Cyclades), Dion (in
Macedonia) and the Asklepieion on
Kos. To them pilgrims of high and
low estate would come from every
corner of the Greek world to pray to
the god for help or oracular advice.
At the Panhellenic festivals, usually
held every four years, huge crowds
flocked to these sanctuaries together
with athletes, physicians, musicians,
poets, actors and traders from near
and far, to exchange ideas and
merchandise, to perform their arts or
to take part in athletic, musical and
poetry competitions. Great religious
gatherings like the Olympic, Pythian,
Nemean and Isthmian festivals and
the Eleusinian Mysteries involved far
more than collective acts of worship:
they were the biggest social occasions
in the ancient world.

LAYOUT OF ANCIENT SANCTUARIES

The two basic essentials of a sanctuary were a walled enclosure (peribolos) and an altar at which libations and sacrifices were offered up. When the cult became more popular and was adopted by the city, a temple was usually built near the altar to house the cult statue. Other structures necessary for cult practices and associated activities, such as theatres and stadia for musical, theatrical and athletic competitions, were then erected round about, often some distance away. The layout of the sanctuary did not necessarily follow a preordained plan but was determined by the lie of the land and other practical considerations. Secular buildings providing facilities for visitors (restaurants, inns, dwelling-houses, etc.) were usually sited outside the sacred precinct: in some places they were so numerous that they formed sizable towns.

A type of building characteristic of ancient sanctuaries was the treasury, used for storing valuable offerings from cities. There would also be hundreds of votive offerings from individual worshippers: sometimes small buildings, more often statues, valuable artefacts or stone blocks bearing grateful inscriptions, set on pedestals in designated parts of the sanctuary.

Since sanctuaries contained precious offerings, often of untold value, they had to be guarded against predators. Many of them, especially those situated a long way away from the nearest town, were therefore protected by high walls with a monumental entrance gate (propylon), which offered further scope for architectural and artistic creativity. The Propylaia of the Acropolis in Athens, designed by Mnesikles, was so widely famed for its beauty that it was copied 400 years later at the Sanctuary of Eleusis.

Olympia

One large Panhellenic shrine which had all the typical sanctuary buildings is Olympia (2). Dominating the scene was the Temple of Zeus in the centre, with the older Temple of Hera to the north, the conical altar between the two, and valuable offerings donated by cities and individuals all around. The whole of this area was enclosed by a peribolos wall with a small propylon, while the treasuries and sundry other buildings serving a variety of purposes were situated outside the peribolos. The treasuries stood in a row at the foot of the Hill of Kronos; to the east were the Stoa of Agnaptos (the "Echo Colonnade") and the Stadium; to the south the Bouleuterion and the South Stoa; at the south-west corner the Leonidaion (a large hotel for wealthy visitors); and north of that the Palaistra and Gymnasium.

The Amphiareion: a healing centre

A smaller but still important sanctuary, comprising all the usual buildings and some other, more specialized ones as well, was the Amphiareion at Oropos in Attica. It was dedicated to the demigod Amphiaraos, a physician and healer, whose cult was at first purely local. As time went by, however, the fame of the miraculous cures wrought at his shrine spread all over the Greek world, with the result that money poured in and many splendid buildings and votive monuments were erected.

The Amphiareion extends over both banks of the narrow valley of a

2

seasonal torrent (1). On the left bank was the sanctuary proper, containing the religious buildings. The altar stood beside a sacred spring, which was apparently the original centre of the cult. Just above that was the temple, with the cult statue in the central aisle. At the east end of the sanctuary were bath-houses (separate for men and women), as patients wishing to be cured had first to wash in spring water to purify the body and soul.

The actual healing process took place at night. After sacrificing a ram, the patient went to sleep wrapped in its fleece in a long stoa which served as an *enkoimeterion* ("oracular dormitory"), awaiting the revelations to be made to him by Amphiaraos in his dreams, which would be interpreted by the priests the next morning. This process was known as *enkoimesis* ("incubation").

Treatment was continued with a cycle of theatrical or musical performances relating to the cult of Amphiaraos, which took place in the theatre behind the *enkoimeterion*. Their purpose was to relieve the patients' stress, give them spiritual and intellectual uplift and reinforce their faith.

The open space between the temple and the *enkoimeterion* was occupied by a row of votive offerings, mainly statues and inscriptions.

On the right bank of the stream, in an area that seems to have developed unplanned, were all the facilities for the pilgrims' bodily needs: shops, inns, a water-clock and many other

smaller buildings.

The altar was the place – not necessarily a built-up structure – where worshippers communicated with their god in what amounted to a process of exchange. They offered up libations of milk or wine, offerings of fruit, nuts or cakes, or sacrifices of animals or birds such as goats, sheep, cocks, oxen, bulls or pigs, according to their means and the preferences of the god concerned (1). In return they asked for help, protection, a good crop or purgation of the guilt of murder or other offences.

Sacrifices

Sacrificial rites were the supreme acts of religious observance. Sacrifices were offered up on the altar, which usually stood in front of the east end of the temple in sight of the cult statue in the temple itself.

The worshippers stood round the altar praying, either standing upright with their arms raised to heaven or bending low in obeisance. After the sacrifice the victim was carved up and roasted on the altar, and the meat was then distributed among the congregation. For them this was the high point of the proceedings, because they were partaking of the consecrated victim that had been offered to the god and at the same time were eating a succulent roast of the highest quality, as only the finest beasts were sacrificed. Most people lived on bread, cheese, olives, beans, fruit, nuts and the occasional fish, so this was a rare opportunity to eat meat.

Evolution of the altar

In Minoan Crete and Mycenaean Greece there were altars of many different types, from small rectangular slabs on a low base to full-sized tables like the one depicted on a Cretan sarcophagus from Ayia Triadha (2). In the sixth, fifth and fourth centuries altars were either small stone tables decorated with reliefs or paintings (1) or larger rectangular blocks of stone of a size proportionate to the size of the temple.

A typical example is the Altar of the Chians, east of the Temple of Apollo at Delphi.
Later, monumental edifices were built to serve as altars. The Altar of Zeus at Pergamon in Asia Minor (3), built by King Eumenes II *circa* 180-160 B.C., was celebrated not only for its enormous size but also for the reliefs on its walls. A hundred years earlier, at Syracuse in Sicily, Hieron II had built an altar 200 metres long (4), not because he had so many requests to make of the gods but because he was a ruler who wanted to be remembered by grandiose construction projects.

Altars were to be found everywhere: in domestic courtyards, market-places, public buildings, temples; above ground for the gods of the heavens, in caves and underground rooms for the gods of the underworld. Every human activity had its own patron deity with his or her own altar, and evidently the gods' favours were much in demand, for we know that the altars were piled high with ash and the bones and horns of sacrificial victims.

3

4

77

Houses of the gods

To the ancient Greeks, temples were the most important buildings of all. A temple had to be worthy of the greatness of the god or goddess whose cult statue was housed there for protection from the elements and defilement by birds.

The temple was the private abode of the god: no mortals were allowed to set foot in it except the priests and a few others who had won themselves the privilege by generous benefactions to the sanctuary. Since most people never went inside, the architects naturally took pains to make the exterior as beautiful and magnificent as possible, not only to honour the god but also to be admired by the public (1). In the interior, which was plain and unadorned, the focus of attention was the cult statue, usually made either or marble or else of wood covered with gold, ivory and other precious materials. The interior was dark and mysterious, with no light except what came in through the door (when it was open) and, in a few temples, through small windows on either side of the door.

It is easy to imagine the jostling for position that must have gone on at a sacrifice, when the temple door was open and everybody in the congregation would have been trying to stand where they could see the statue of the god glinting in the occasional rays of sunlight that fell on it.

2

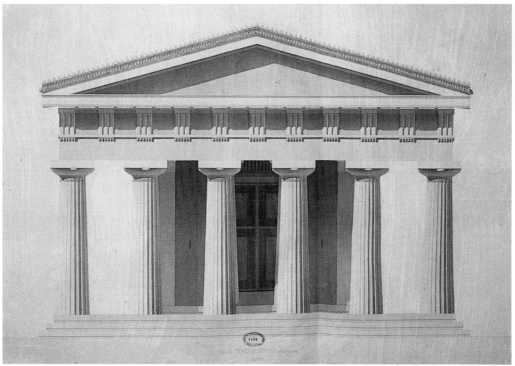

3

General principles
of temple design

The history of temple architecture is
quite straightforward.
The ground plan of the earliest
Greek temples was based on that of
the Mycenaean megaron (the main
hall of a Mycenaean palace,
consisting of the throne room
preceded by a smaller anteroom with
a pillared porch) (2). Some idea of
what an early temple looked like is
given by surviving clay models, like
this one found at Argos (3).
It was in the seventh century B.C. that
the Greeks started building
monumental temples, although large
temple-shaped buildings are known
from earlier than that. The technical
improvements and architectural

developments of the ensuing century
remained in use for a thousand years
thereafter.
The main differences between
temples are differences of type, size,
architectural order and proportion
(4). According to Vitruvius, the basic
principles of temple architecture were
symmetry and proportion. Ancient
architects paid such meticulous
attention to detail that archaeologists
today can calculate the exact size of a
temple, the number of its columns
and other particulars even if there is
nothing left of it but part of one
column drum.

I

TYPES OF TEMPLE

In its simplest form the temple was merely a rectangular room called the *sekos* (*cella*) with a door at one end. At the entrance there was often a small porch with two or more columns between *antae*, which are forward extensions of the side walls of the sekos. This type is known as a temple *in antis* (1, 2). The type with a porch supported by a row of free-standing columns, with or without antae behind them, is called a *prostyle* temple (3). Since the ancient Greeks liked symmetry in architecture, they sometimes built temples with a similar porch at the back as well: this type is called an *amphiprostyle* temple (4).

A major innovation was the addition of a *peristyle*, a colonnade running round the entire building and forming a covered walk (the *pteron*) between it and the temple wall. A temple with a peristyle is a *peripteral* temple (5), a type which exists in various forms. If it is surrounded by not one but two rows of columns it is called *dipteral* (6): the double colonnade is found in a number of

particularly grand temples of the Archaic and Classical periods on Samos and in the big Greek cities of Asia Minor.

The number of columns in the peristyle of a peripteral temple depended on their size, but there was a constant ratio between the number of columns at each end and on each side. In the Classical period the number of columns along each side was always double the number at each end, plus one. The Temple of Hephaistos in Athens (7) has 6×13 columns, the Parthenon 8×17. There are also variations in the ground plan of the temple building itself. In the Archaic period the sekos was very often divided into two aisles by a longitudinal interior colonnade (8). In Classical times there was often an interior Π-shaped colonnade surrounding the cult statue on three sides: this feature is found in the Parthenon and also in the Temple of Hephaistos, where statues of Hephaistos and Athena stood together on a raised platform decorated with reliefs (9).

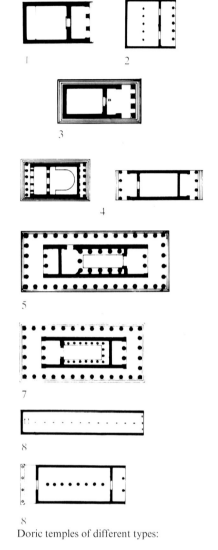

Doric temples of different types:

1. Of Dionysos at Miletos (1st qtr. of the 3rd c. B.C.)
2. Of Demeter at Sangri, Naxos (*c.* 530 B.C.)
3. Of Demeter at Miletos (2nd half of the 3rd c. B.C.)
4. (Left) Of Apollo at Delos (425-417 B.C.)
   (Right) Of Athena at Lindos (*c.* 300 B.C.)
5. Of Apollo at Bassai (*c.* 425 B.C.)
6. Of Apollo at Didyma (*c.* 300 B.C.)
7. Of Hephaistos (the "Theseion") in Athens (449-420 B.C.)
8. (Upper) Heraion I at Samos (1st half of the 8th c. B.C.)(Lower) Oikos of the Naxians at Delos (early 6th c. B.C.)

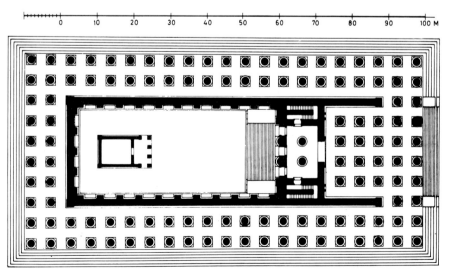

7

PLAN OF THE TEMPLE OF APOLLO AT CORINTH (6th c. B.C.)

1. Stylobate
2. Stepped krepis
3. Pronaos
4. Cella

5. Adyton
6. Opisthodomos
7. Pteron
8. Anta

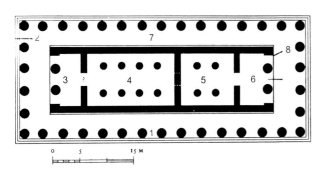

9

1

All ancient Greek temples (and other monumental buildings too, of course) had massive foundations going down to solid rock or at least to a firm subsoil. The whole of this substructure was called the *stereobate*. The top level of the stereobate, the *euthynteria*, projected slightly above ground and was the lowest visible part of the temple. On top of the stereobate was the *krepis* or *krepidoma*, which usually consisted of three stepped courses of solid stone. Its purpose was to provide a firm base for the building to rest on and to raise it into a more commanding position, as with the Temple of Poseidon at Sounion (1). The uppermost step of the *krepis* – the platform on which the temple actually rested – was called the *stylobate*.

TEMPLE OF ATHENA
APHAIA ON AIGINA
(500-480 B.C.)

DORIC ORDER

1. Stepped krepis
2. Fluting
3. Temple door
4. Capital
5. Architrave
6. Frieze
7. Cramp (cramp-iron)
8. Ceiling
9. Entablature
10. Coffers
11. Guttae
12. Mutules
13. Sima
14. Raked cornice
15. Akroterion
16. Horizontal cornice
17. Triglyph
18. Metope
19. Regula
20. Taenia
21. Abacus
22. Echinos

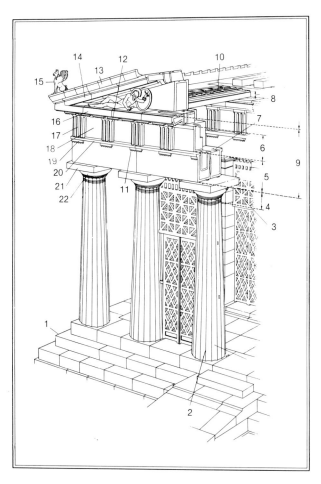

The two predominant architectural orders in ancient Greek temples were the Doric (found chiefly in mainland Greece, southern Italy and Sicily) and the Ionic (in Asia Minor and the Aegean islands). The Doric is weightier, more massive, with a rather heavy entablature, the Ionic airier and more graceful, with a lighter superstructure. Apart from the differences in the proportions of the columns and the design of the capitals, the main distinction between them is that in the Doric order the frieze consists of alternating triglyphs and metopes, whereas in the Ionic it is a continuous band surmounted by a row of dentils.

Columns

In most orders the columns were composed of three sections: the *base*, the *shaft* and the *capital*. A Doric column had no base but rested directly on the stylobate. Sometimes the shaft was monolithic, but more often it consisted of a number of *drums*. Columns were *fluted*, that is to say their circular outline was indented all round with shallow rounded furrows (flutes) running vertically from top to bottom. In the Doric order the flutes were separated by sharp edges (arrises), in the Ionic order by flat strips (fillets).
The column capitals supported the *architrave*, a horizontal stone beam, plain in the Doric order, divided into three shallow slabs in the Ionic. Above the architrave was the *frieze*, which in the Ionic order is a continuous band of stone (often sculptured) but in the Doric is composed of triglyphs and metopes (the latter often sculptured). Above the frieze was the horizontal *cornice*,

which projected beyond the frieze and architrave and protected them from the weather.
The architrave, frieze and cornice together comprise the *entablature*.

Pediments

At each end of the temple the roof terminated in a triangular *pediment*. The recessed space bounded by the *raked cornices* of the pediment and

the horizontal cornice of the entablature beneath was the *tympanum*, which was usually filled with *pedimental statuary*.
The *sima* was a gutter along the top of the raked cornices to prevent rainwater from spilling over on to the pediment.
At each corner of the pediment there stood an *akroterion*, a sculptural ornament that might be a floral design or a statue.

DORIC

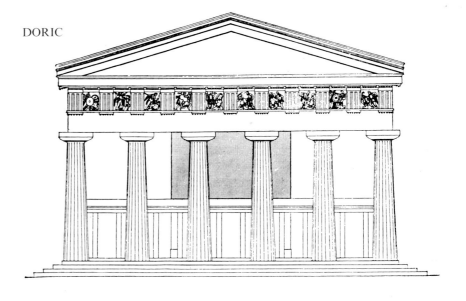

IONIC

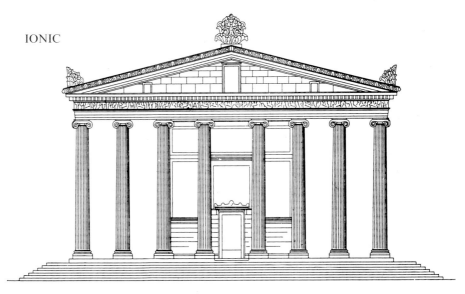

COLUMN CAPITALS

The capital is the topmost element of the column, taking the weight of the architrave. At first, in the seventh and sixth centuries, they were of two main types, *Doric* (1) and *Ionic* (2), according to the architectural style of the temple. The *Aeolic* capital (4) was also found in the same period, but more rarely than the others. A type that became very prevalent from the fourth century B.C. was the *Corinthian* capital (3), used with the Ionic order, and in the Hellenistic period various new types were introduced, such as the *Pergamene* (5) and the *Egyptizing*, among others. The Doric capital has the simplest and cleanest lines of them all. It consists of the *abacus* (a plain square slab) with the *echinos* (a basin-shaped circular moulding) below. The earliest form of the echinos resembled the shell of a sea-urchin, from which it took its name.

The Ionic capital also had an abacus above and an echinos below, but the middle section was adorned with a pair of *volutes* (spiral scrolls resembling ram's horns), which are its most distinctive feature.

The Corinthian capital consists of an abacus and a *calathus* (Gk. *kalathos*, basket), which is the principal member of the Corinthian capital, shaped like an inverted bell. The calathus is adorned with three overlapping rows of scrolling acanthus leaves and other foliate motifs.

Sometimes statues of women (Caryatids) (6) or men (Atlantes) were used instead of columns.

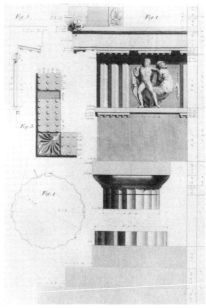

1

2

7

8

3

5

6

9

4

THE PARTHENON

The Temple of Athena Parthenos on the Acropolis of Athens is the supreme masterpiece of ancient Greek architecture and one of the most eloquent expressions of the human creative genius. At the same time it is the most evocative monument of Classical Greek civilization, because it is inseparably linked with the time and conditions of its creation. It was the product of a unique combination of circumstances: a flourishing democracy, a population brimming with enthusiasm and creative exuberance after resounding victories over a powerful invader, a treasury with full coffers and the simultaneous presence of far-sighted statesmen, gifted artists and skilled craftsmen, all of whom helped to make the temple what it is.

The credit for the building of the Classical Parthenon belongs to Perikles and his entourage of scholars and artists. In about 450 B.C. Perikles submitted a motion to the Ekklesia (Assembly of Citizens) proposing that Athenian Confederacy funds be used for the reconstruction of the temples and other monuments destroyed by the Persians thirty years earlier. The building programme he had in mind was part of his broader policy of making Athens a resplendent capital city of the entire Greek world. His first concern, naturally, was to build a splendid temple in honour of the city's patron goddess.

The project is launched

As soon as the Ekklesia had approved the project, Iktinos and Kallikrates were appointed to draw up the architectural plans, while Perikles's friend Pheidias was commissioned to make the chryselephantine statue of Athena for the new temple and was put in overall charge of the project. However, since everything had to be done in accordance with Athenian law, the finances were put under the supervision of a controlling committee whose members were appointed for a one-year term and were answerable to the Ekklesia. The committee was responsible for the purchase of materials and the payment of wages, salaries and all other expenses. At the end of their term the outgoing committee members handed over the funds to their successors and recorded on marble stelai all the jobs of work that had been done during their period in office and the amount spent on each. Thanks to these inscriptions we know that the quarrying of Pentelic marble for the Parthenon started in 447/6, that the construction of the building was completed in the remarkably short time of ten years and that by 433/2 all the sculptural decoration was in place. It is thought that most of the Athenian citizens worked on the project, either voluntarily or for money.

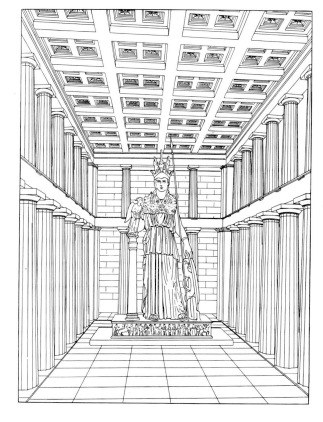

3

1

Description of the building

It can be seen from the plan (2) that the Parthenon is a Doric octastyle peripteral temple, with eight columns at each end and seventeen along each side (the corner columns being counted twice). The sekos was divided into two rooms of unequal size. The one on the east was the larger and had a two-tiered, Π-shaped, interior Doric colonnade of 23 columns surrounding the statue of Athena Parthenos (3). In the western room, which was accessible only from the opisthodomos, there were four tall Ionic columns supporting the roof.

The Parthenon was one of the biggest Classical Greek temples. For the construction of such a massive edifice

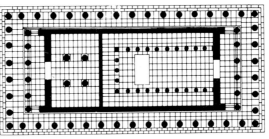

2

3

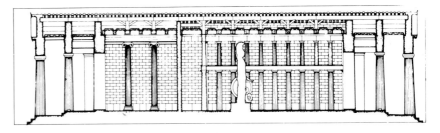

enormous quantities of stone were required, even though the builders made use of the existing substructure of an earlier temple, the Old Parthenon, which had been destroyed by the Persians before it was completed.

Apart from the wooden ceiling the entire building, even including the roof tiles, was of Pentelic marble. It has been calculated that about 13,400 blocks of stone of various sizes were used in its construction. More astonishing still, no two of these blocks are exactly the same: every one differs from every other, even those immediately adjacent to it, either in size – the variations between them being minute – or in shape. This is due to the optical *refinements* (see below). Yet in spite of these imperceptible differences and in spite of their size (some of them weigh 5-10 tons), they fit together perfectly: in fact the precision of the measurements down to the last detail, even in places that will never be seen, is one of the most amazing features of the whole building. The Greeks' mastery of high-precision stone-cutting techniques and the skills of their masons reached a higher pitch in this period than at any time before or since.

Aesthetic qualities

The Parthenon's distinction as a work of art is due to a great many carefully worked-out aesthetic qualities, which can be classified under two headings:
(a) The *proportions* of its surfaces and masses, and
(b) The *refinements* applied in its construction.

Proportions

The Parthenon is 69.50 m. long by 30.88 m. wide, a ratio of approximately 9:4. The same ratio is repeated in the dimensions of smaller parts of the building, including the width to the height of the façade (excluding the pediment) at each end. Thus the component parts of the temple stand in a harmonious relationship to each other, with none of them dominating or overpowering

any of the others. Another factor of great importance to the sense of graceful proportion it conveys is its position on the Acropolis: the first view one has of it on emerging from the Propylaia is from the north-west, from where one sees all three dimensions – height, length and breadth – in perfect relationship to each other, without actually being aware of the unseen subtleties in the proportions of the building as a whole and of its parts to one another.

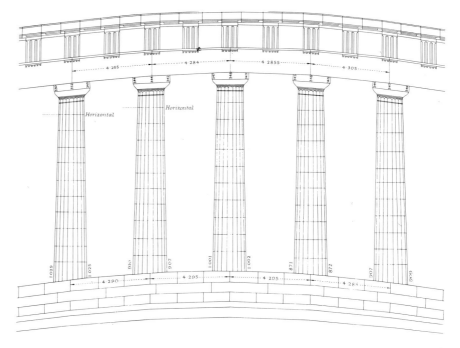

4

Refinements

The Parthenon was not the first building to incorporate architectural refinements, that is to say the imperceptible curvature of what appear to be horizontal and vertical straight lines, for such optical tricks had been used in Greece since the Archaic period. But it is in the Parthenon that these refinements are to be seen in full perfection.

The refinements are present throughout the building, from the stylobate up. The stylobate has a slight convex curve along all four sides (4), giving a rise of 11 cm. from the corners to the centre of each long side and 7 cm. to the centre of each short side. This curvature is repeated in all the horizontal elements of the entablature.

Similarly, the vertical lines of the building are neither vertical nor always straight. The columns, which appear to taper towards the top, in fact have a convex *entasis*, or swelling, reaching their maximum breadth about one-third of the way up and then tapering from there to the capital. Nor are they absolutely vertical, for they lean very slightly inwards on all four sides of the temple (which means that the corner columns are inclined towards the centre of the building). The inward slant of the columns is imparted to the walls of the sekos.

There are also variations in the intercolumniation, the end columns being slightly closer together and those near the middle more widely spaced.

It is clear from all this that the differences and divergences are not just *ad hoc* corrective measures but a comprehensive system of imperceptible modifications that extends through the whole temple, binding its component parts together and adjusting their aesthetic balance. One result of these imperceptible touches is that there are no straight lines in the Parthenon. All the optical refinements, deliberately exaggerated for the sake of clarity, are illustrated in the sketch below (5).

The refinements serve the purely aesthetic purpose of imparting life and buoyancy to the building, which would not be the case if all the lines were absolutely straight and all the surfaces absolutely flat.

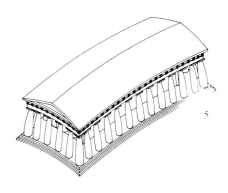

1

Tholoi

While most ancient Greek buildings were rectangular, tholoi or rotundas were sometimes found in the agora of a city and quite often in large sanctuaries. Those built in the fourth century B.C. were the most impressive both in size and in appearance, as they were lavishly decorated with reliefs and paintings. The most widely famed in antiquity were the Philippeion at Olympia (which contained the statues of Alexander the Great's family), the Tholos in the Sanctuary of Athena Pronaia at Delphi and the Tholos at Epidauros. The last of these, generally considered one of the loveliest buildings in ancient Greece (1), was built by Polykleitos, the architect of the Epidauros theatre. A peristyle of 26 Doric columns encircling the wall of the Tholos supported the entablature with its triglyphs and sculptured metopes. The roof was crowned by a sima adorned with palmettes and lion's-head gargoyles. An interior ring of fourteen columns with beautiful Corinthian capitals supported the carved coffered ceiling (2), and the floor was paved in chequerboard fashion with black and white lozenge-shaped marble slabs (3). Although it is possible to reconstruct the appearance of the Tholos at Epidauros, its purpose (like that of other tholoi) remains obscure. Various hypotheses have been put forward: that it was used for orgiastic mystery rites, or for subterranean libations to chthonic deities, or even that it housed the sacred snakes of Asklepios which played an important part in the sanctuary's ritual healing processes.

2

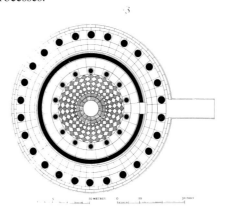

Telesteria

Side by side with the official religion there existed a few mystery cults which had started as primitive rites but gradually evolved into esoteric religious systems which met people's need for spiritual comfort and gave them hope of a life after death. The biggest mystery cult was based at Eleusis and was connected with the sowing, cultivation and harvesting of wheat, skills which Demeter and Persephone were said to have taught to the human race. The rituals – a series of initiation ceremonies and other rites about which little is known – took place in large hypostyle halls known as telesteria.

The Telesterion (Hall of the Mysteries) at Eleusis (4) originated in the Mycenaean era as the *Anaktoron*, which was retained as the "holy of holies" in all the later buildings erected on the site. The ruins visible today are those of the Telesterion of the fourth century B.C. (5), which was a large hall, almost square, with tiers of seats on all four sides for the initiates attending the rites. The roof was supported on 42 columns and had a lantern in the centre. There were no windows, and the six doorways (two each on three of the four sides) were narrow, so the lantern in the roof was virtually the only source of daylight and air. Further light was provided by flaming torches, creating an atmosphere of mystery that was heightened by the forest of columns (6). The worshippers would no doubt have been watching with bated breath as the hierophants (priests) emerged from the anaktoron carrying the sacred symbols of the cult.

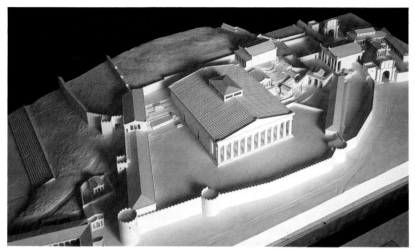

4

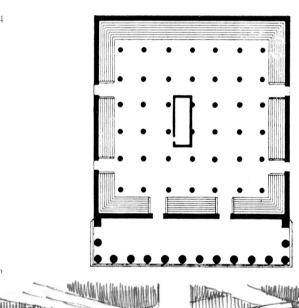

5

6

No temple was complete without the sculptures that adorned it and helped to give it its distinctive character. Some discussion of sculpture therefore has a rightful place here, not with the idea of tracing its development but to show what purposes were served by sculpture in temple architecture, taking the Parthenon as an example.

The sculptural decoration of a temple performed three functions. The first was ornamental: it beautified surfaces that would otherwise have been plain and unadorned. The second was religious: the sculptures usually illustrated incidents from the life of the god concerned, or exploits attributed to him. And the third was political or ideological: very often the mythological subjects depicted on pediments or friezes were intended as allegories of events in the city's history or of its political ideology.

Sculptural ornamentation of the Parthenon

The Parthenon's sculptural ornamentation is worthy of its architecture in quality, quantity and subject matter; a fitting culmination of the grand designs of Perikles and his associates. The planning of Perikles's building programme was under the overall charge of Pheidias, who was assisted in its execution by many other sculptors including some of his ablest pupils.

The metopes

The Parthenon was the first Greek temple to have figural reliefs on all of its metopes, of which there were 92 (14 at each end and 32 along each side). Each face of the building dealt with a different mythological story, illustrated in serial form with two or occasionally three figures on each metope: the Gigantomachy on the east, the sack of Troy on the north, the Centauromachy on the south and the Amazonomachy on the west. All these mythical subjects were allusions to the Athenians' recent victories over the Persians.

WEST PEDIMENT OF THE PARTHENON

1. River Kephisos or Ilissos, or a hero
2. Kekrops
3. Wife or daughter of Kekrops
4. Daughter of Kekrops
5. Erysichthon
6. Daughter of Kekrops
7. Nike (Victory)
8. Hermes
9. Athena's chariot
10. Athena
11. Poseidon
12. Poseidon's chariot
13. Iris
14. Amphitrite or Thetis on a sea monster
15. Oreithyia
16. Ion
17. Kreousa
18, 19. Daughters of Erechtheus
20. A river or Kephalos
21. Kallirrhoe or Prokris

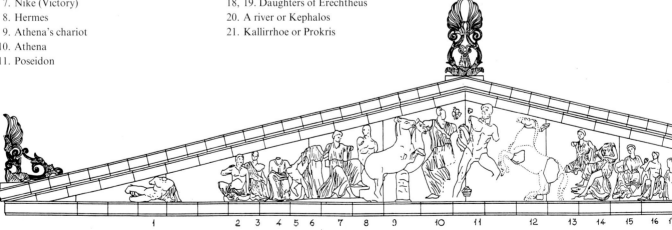

The Ionic frieze

The subject of the continuous or Ionic frieze of the Parthenon (as opposed to the Doric frieze composed of metopes interrupted by triglyphs) was the procession of the Great Panathenaia, a four-yearly festival in honour of the city's patron goddess Athena. The citizens turned out *en masse* with their wives and children and joined the procession on foot or on horseback, escorting the magistrates and priests who brought Athena's new peplos from the Pompeion (near the Dipylon Gate) to the Acropolis.

The reliefs illustrated all three stages of the procession. On the west face were the preparations and the marshalling of the participants. Both the side faces depicted the procession under way, with chariots, horsemen, musicians, civic dignitaries and the sacrificial animals. At the east end was the religious rite at which the peplos was handed over to the goddess, watched by the twelve Olympian gods and goddesses in two groups.

The frieze was 1 m. high and had a total length of 160 m. Although the figures are in low relief, the breadth of conception and the quality of the workmanship are quite astonishing (2).

The pediments

The two pediments contained about fifty statues, made between 437 and 432, in groups representing mythological scenes connected with Athens' great patron goddess, who was worshipped in the temple. In the centre of the east pediment, over the main entrance, was the miraculous birth of Athena, who sprang fully armed from Zeus's head. Ranged on either side were the rest of the Olympian gods, dumbstruck with amazement at this extraordinary event. In the centre of the west pediment was the contest between Athena and Poseidon for supremacy over the city. To left and right of the two central figures and the chariots which had brought them to the Acropolis were the first kings and mythical heroes of Athens (Kekrops, Erechtheus and others), watching and judging the contest (1).

Coffered ceilings

The interior ceilings of temples were usually made of wood, but in the pteron (the roofed walk between the sekos walls and the surrounding peristyle) the ceiling was of marble slabs resting on stout stone beams. The underside of each slab was recessed to form a coffer which was adorned with decorative designs, either painted or in relief, often with a floral ornament of gilded metal in the centre.

2

1

21

93

Eliminating our preconceptions

Because the ruined Greek temples we see today are of stark white marble, we tend to think they were always like that; but they were not. Colour was an important expressive medium in ancient Greek art, and it would have been unthinkable for the Greeks not to use it in their temples. In fact, certain parts of every temple were always painted in many colours. Little of the original colour has survived to the present day, of course, but many more traces of paint were visible even as late as the nineteenth century, when it was fashionable to reconstruct the original appearance of ancient monuments, allowing free rein to the imagination where necessary. A number of French architecture students of that time did in fact produce vivid full-colour reconstructions of ancient Greek temples as they envisaged them.

Techniques and colours

On temples built of porous limestone it was easy to apply the paint on the white plaster that covered the whole building, and on the terracotta elements of the entablature (metopes, sima, cornices, etc.). But for painting on marble the *encaustic* technique was used: the pigment was mixed into melted wax, which was applied to the marble either in blocks of solid colour or wherever it was needed for the chosen design. It was then polished all over with a hot iron, which fused the pigmented wax on to the surface and drove the colour deep into the pores of the marble. All the sculptures – the pedimental statuary as well as the frieze reliefs – were originally painted in variegated colours. The triglyphs were always dark blue, as were the tympana of the pediments. Red was used for the background of the metopes and certain parts of the column capitals. All the decoratively carved mouldings of the entablature were picked out in dark blue, red and gold, and the same colours were used for the coffers of the ceilings. The outer walls of the sekos were generally red, a colour that went well with the ornamental bronze facings of the doors and the bronze balustrades (for there were often balustrades blocking the gaps between columns). It would appear that the shafts of the columns were sometimes painted, too, either in light grey or pale yellow ochre, partly in order to tone down the dazzling white of the bare marble and partly to cover over the horizontal interstices between column drums and the grain of the marble so as to give the column a smoother, more uniform appearance.

All things that are made have their makers. Civilization and progress would be impossible without all the people – theoreticians, artists and craftsmen – who have wrestled with the problems, mastered the technical or artistic skills available to them and given shape to their raw materials. Many ancient Greek architects' names have been preserved by tradition and history, others have been forgotten. Sometimes we know the name of the man who invented a new technique or process without knowing how people had managed until then. Some wrote books about their work. The books exist no more, but we are still left with ruined buildings, names and countless myths. Let us take a look at the personalities of certain ancient architects and the nature of their work.

Daidalos, first of the great inventors

Daidalos, whose name means "cunningly made" or "clever artificer", is mentioned in the *Iliad* as a great craftsman. According to later myths and writers such as Apollodoros, Virgil and Pausanias, he was the designer of the Labyrinth, which probably preserves an ancestral memory of the maze-like palace of Knossos. He was born in Athens, the son of Eupalamos ("Dexterous") and Phrasimede ("Deep Thinker") and worked there as a sculptor of statues until the Areopagus condemned him to exile for the murder of a particularly able pupil of his. He took refuge in Crete with King Minos, who commissioned him to design his palace, but there his skill as a craftsman got him into

1

trouble: to satisfy the abominable lust of Pasiphae, Minos's wife, he made a hollow wooden cow that was so lifelike that Poseidon's bull was deceived by it and mounted Pasiphae, who was hidden inside. The monstrous fruit of that union was the man-eating Minotaur. Minos reacted leniently, merely confining the Minotaur in the Labyrinth, but his fury knew no bounds when Daidalos helped Theseus to kill the Minotaur. Daidalos and his son Ikaros were then imprisoned in the Labyrinth themselves; however, Daidalos made two pairs of wings out of feathers and wax, with which both of them escaped. He himself flew to Sicily, where he is said to have built the city walls of Akragas, the Temple of Aphrodite at Eryx and a bath-house at Selinous. Tradition has it that another Daidalos was the sculptor of the earliest big Greek statues in the seventh century B.C. What connection there was between him and his prehistoric namesake, and whether either of them was a real person, we can only guess. The fact remains that the name of Daidalos spans a period of about a thousand years and was associated by the ancient Greeks with many of the earliest achievements in architecture, sculpture and technology.

2

It is interesting to see that the device which the people of Knossos used on their coins in historical times was a diagram of the Labyrinth (1), although they could never have seen even the ruins of the Minoan palace (2), which by then had lain buried for centuries.

Hippodamos, planner and philosopher

Hippodamos, born at Miletos in Asia Minor, lived and worked in Athens during the "Golden Age" of the fifth century. There he was well known, not only for his unconventional appearance (long-haired and garishly dressed) but also for the originality of his thinking, which he applied in the field of architecture and planning. Central to his philosophy was his vision of an ideal city with not more than 40,000 inhabitants, in which equality and justice for all would be the rule. The population would be divided into three classes – artisans, farmers and soldiers – and the land likewise, with privately-owned land for the farmers, state-owned land to provide revenue to pay the soldiers, and consecrated land for the gods.

In the cities that Hippodamos planned, the streets were laid out in a rectangular grid composed of blocks of uniform size and shape. All the administrative offices were in the Agora, while the shops and sanctuaries were in clearly demarcated zones nearby. His own birthplace, Miletos, was the first city to be laid out in this way (3). In Piraeus, which was rebuilt in accordance with the Hippodamian plan on the initiative of the Athenian authorities, excavators have found some of the boundary stones marking the divisions between the different zones of the city.

To back up his ideas on town planning, Hippodamos proposed a package of legislation granting all citizens equality in the eyes of the law.

Once the new city of Piraeus had been built, Hippodamos, along with such other well-known figures as Herodotos and the philosopher Protagoras, joined the expedition to found Athens' one and only colony in southern Italy, Thourioi or Thurii: his job was to supervise its planning and construction. His last project, undertaken at the end of his long life, was the master plan for the city of Rhodes, which excavation has shown to have been laid out in accordance with his precepts.

Cities with rectangular grid plans existed before Hippodamos, but he was the first person to apply an integrated theory of planning and construction based on the principles of democracy and equal rights.

3

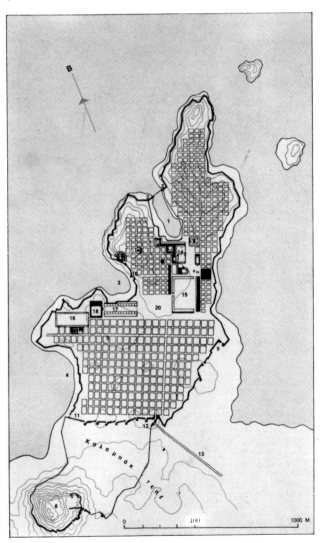

Deinokrates, a landscape architect

Deinokrates was a Macedonian whose physical bearing was as majestic as his ideas – and his buildings – were breathtakingly grand. It was through the combination of these qualities that he managed to attract the attention of Alexander the Great. The story goes that when Alexander was judging a lawsuit somewhere in Asia Minor, Deinokrates appeared before him naked, with a wreath of poplar leaves on his head, a lion-skin over his shoulder and a club in his hand. Alexander halted the proceedings to ask who he was. "A Macedonian architect who begs to offer you some ideas and plans worthy of your majesty," Deinokrates answered. "O King, I have devised a scheme for the development of Mount Athos: the whole mountain will be sculpted in the form of a colossal human figure holding in his left hand a great fortified city and in his right a lake catching the water from all the springs on the mountain, from which a great waterfall will cascade into the sea." Alexander rejected the idea because there would be no farmland near the city, but he kept Deinokrates on as his adviser and, on reaching Egypt, instructed him to build the new city of Alexandria. This Deinokrates did, creating a city of unrivalled grandeur. Two other projects attributed to him are the Temple of Artemis (4, 5) built at Ephesos to replace the one burnt down in 325 B.C., and a grand monument to Alexander's friend Hephaistion that was erected at Babylon.

4

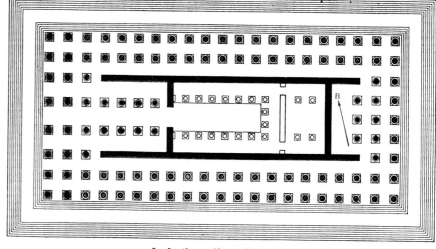

5

0 5 10   20   30   40 M.

Vitruvius, *De Architectura*

Marcus Vitruvius Pollio, a Roman architect and engineer who lived in the first century B.C., wrote the only treatise on architecture that has come down to us from antiquity. In it he drew on the work of Greek writers on architecture such as Hermogenes (3rd cent. B.C.), who in turn had drawn on earlier sources. *De Architectura*, as Vitruvius's work is entitled, is divided into ten books which are a mine of theoretical, practical and historical information on ancient Greek architecture as well as the author's views on the personal and professional standards appropriate to an architect. Not only was Vitruvius's work the only reliable handbook for his contemporaries, but it also had an enormous influence on Renaissance architecture 1,300 years later (6).

Numerous manuscript copies of it had survived the Middle Ages, and it was first printed at Rome in 1486. In Book VII of *De Architectura* Vitruvius mentions a number of ancient architects who wrote books about their work: "Agatharchus, in Athens, when Aeschylus was bringing out a tragedy, painted a scene, and left a commentary about it. This led Democritus and Anaxagoras to write on the same subject, showing how, given a centre in a definite place, the lines should naturally correspond with due regard to the point of sight and the divergence of the visual rays, so that by this deception a faithful representation of the appearance of buildings might be given in painted scenery. Afterwards Silenus published a book on the proportions of Doric structures; Theodorus, on the Doric temple of Juno which is in Samos; Chersiphron and Metagenes, on the Ionic temple at Ephesus which is Diana's; ... Ictinus and Carpion, on the Doric temple of Minerva [the Parthenon] which is on the acropolis of Athens; Theodorus the Phocian, on the Round Building [the Tholos] which is at Delphi; ... on the Mausoleum, Satyrus and Pytheos who were favoured with the greatest and highest good fortune, for men whose artistic talents are believed to have won them the highest renown for all time ... devised and executed works of supreme excellence in this building: ... Leochares, Bryaxis, Scopas, Praxiteles...." Book VII opens with an acknowledgement: "And so the ancients deserve no ordinary, but unending thanks, because they did not pass on in envious silence, but took care that their ideas of every kind should be transmitted to the future in their writings."[6]

99

An architect's qualifications

It was not easy to become an architect in antiquity. Vitruvius says that anyone wishing to practise the profession ought to be well versed in drawing, geometry, history, philosophy, music, medicine, jurisprudence and case law, astronomy and the movements of the heavenly bodies, and all this to a standard higher than that expected of a specialist! "Optics," he explains, "are necessary for his understanding of the lighting of a building, geometry for symmetry and proportion, arithmetic so that he can work out the budget." However, he himself admits that his list of an architect's ideal qualifications is so long that no one person could possibly master them all.

Social status

Little is known about the social origins of architects in antiquity, other than the fact that they came from a variety of backgrounds. Of the hundred or so whose names we know, some were men of good family: most of these were the sons of other architects and sometimes they paid for the whole project themselves, which means that they must have been well off. But it is very likely that some were the sons of artisans, mostly sculptors, as many ancient architects were themselves sculptors as well.

An architect's duties

First of all, the architect drew up the plans and prepared the feasibility study. He had to be architect, civil engineer and mechanical engineer in one, and sometimes building contractor as well, as his constant presence was required when the construction work was in progress.

His responsibilities started at the quarry – for it was up to him to decide how the stone was to be transported, how the blocks were to be lifted, what kind of cranes should be used and sometimes how the cranes themselves were to be constructed – and did not end until every last sculpture and embellishment was in place.

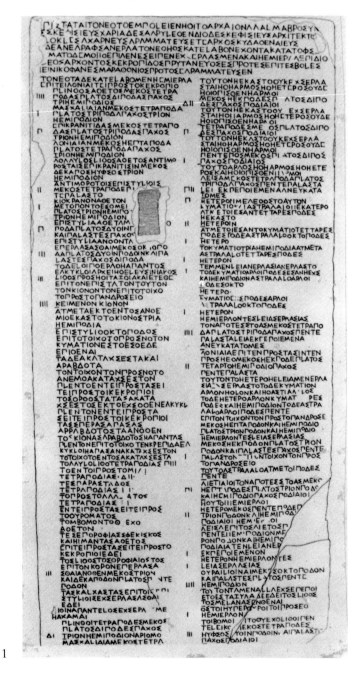

1

Private benefactions

When an individual donor was paying for a project, as in the case of the Stoa of Attalos, the architect was apparently appointed by the benefactor, though it may be that the appointment had to be approved by the civic authorities in that particular case. For the Leonidaion at Olympia, as we have seen, Leonidas of Naxos was not only the donor but also the supervising architect, just as Andronikos Kyrrhestes designed the Tower of the Winds in Athens and paid for its construction.

Funding

The funding of public works projects in Athens was the responsibility of a special committee. The money might come from the spoils of past battles, or from the profits of the state-owned silver mines in a good year, or from the contributions levied from Athens' allies, as in the case of the funds appropriated by Perikles for the building of the Parthenon. Sometimes the architect in charge was authorized to make payments for materials or workers' wages without waiting for the committee's approval.

The size of the jobs for which separate contracts were awarded varied enormously. From the Temple of Asklepios at Epidauros we have contracts for sums ranging from half a drachma to 9,800 drachmai, and elsewhere there were projects budgeted at up to 300 talents: this is the amount Herodotos says was spent on rebuilding the Temple of Apollo at Delphi after the old one had been burnt down in 548 B.C.

Administrative and legal controls

The ancient Greeks were extremely careful about anything to do with the administration of public funds. At Ephesos there was a law in force which, though strict, was perfectly fair in its way: whenever an architect was awarded a public works project he had to submit an estimate of the total cost and deposit his personal fortune as an earnest of good performance. His funds were then held in trust for the city, and if the cost overran the original estimate by 25 per cent or more the city was entitled to keep as much as was necessary to cover the excess. Feasibility studies and budgets were therefore prepared with meticulous care and accuracy.

Awarding the contract

In Athens, the citizens as a whole were responsible for all decisions relating to public works projects. The Ekklesia appointed the architect and set up a five-man committee to monitor the performance of the work and check all expenditures. The architect prepared the plans, made a small model of the completed building and drew up the budget. As regards more detailed working drawings, like those used nowadays, we do not know what the practice was before the Hellenistic period.

Fees

Architects' fees are known to have been between one and two drachmai per day, which was little more than an artisan's wages, so clearly they did not take up the profession for the sake of the money. Presumably they, and the artists who worked with them, chose their careers to gain prestige and the admiration of their fellow-citizens.

Inscriptions - Wages

A full set of plans and drawings was prepared before work started on any project, but there was nothing to prevent changes – sometimes extensive changes – from being made while it was in progress. There are many extant inscriptions recording such changes, and many others giving details of budgets, payroll costs and other expenditures. An inscription of the late fifth century B.C. relating to the building of the Erechtheion in Athens (1) informs us, among other things, that there were 110 persons of all ages and social classes working at a flat rate of pay: one drachma per day.

The materials people use for making ordinary buildings are usually to be found in their immediate environment: stone, mud, tree-trunks, branches, twigs, reeds and so on. The centuries roll by and nothing changes: a simple farm building in Boiotia today (1) differs very little from one built there in prehistoric times. But in more advanced cultures and for more complex structures the materials are often brought from far away and present greater variety: marble for temples, cedarwood beams for their roofs, ivory for ornamentation, lead and iron as mentioned below.

Wood

Wood was the standard material for roofs, ceilings, stairs and door and window frames, just as it has been from prehistoric times to the present day. Hardly any of the wooden parts of ancient buildings have survived because the wood has rotted away, but it is often possible to see where they were, either from the sockets made for them in the masonry or from their imprints in mud or mortar. Archaeological findings about the uses of wood in architecture are corroborated by ancient writings. We also know that the tools used in antiquity – axes, adzes, saws, drills, lathes, planes – were very similar to those of modern times, and the ancient names (in only slightly altered form) are still used in Modern Greek.

Ancient writers also tell us much of what we know about the kinds of trees whose wood was used in architecture. Cedar, which according to Vitruvius lasts for ever and was grown in Crete, around Sikyon in the N. Peloponnese, in Africa and in parts of Syria, was used for roof beams because it has a tall, straight trunk; and the same is true of the cypress. Cedar is known to have been used for the roof of the Odeion of Herodes Atticus in Athens, and cypress for the roof of the Parthenon. Columns and doorsills were often made of oak, ceilings and floors of pine or fir. Cedar was sometimes used for staircases and doors, while olive-wood, walnut and beech had various uses. Luxury furniture and caskets were sometimes veneered with ebony.

The best time of year for felling trees for timber was the autumn. First the bark was slashed, and then the tree was left for a while to drain off some of the sap before it was felled.

Unbaked clay

The principal use of clay in architecture was for the manufacture of bricks, which were shaped in moulds and left out to dry in the sun (unlike roof tiles, which were baked in a kiln). House walls were built of these sun-dried bricks, except for a few courses at the base, and so were the walls of many cities. Some of the bricks used in the wall of Peisistratos enclosing the sanctuary at Eleusis measure 45×45×10 cm. The widespread use of such bricks was due to the fact that they were cheaply and quickly made and easily handled, and they also had a high degree of elasticity which increased their resistance to earthquakes.

The bricks were laid in regular courses, with timbers at intervals to reinforce the structure, and were plastered over for protection from the rain. Fortification walls, which were thicker, were further protected by a roof of tiles along the top.

1

Terracotta

Terracotta, or baked clay, was used for building accessories such as roof tiles, water pipes (2) and gutters. Kiln-baked bricks came into use in Greece in the early Roman period (second century B.C.) and rapidly came to be the predominant building material for all kinds of Roman structures.

Vitruvius recommends that bricks should be made in spring or autumn and not used until two years after they are made, and that they should be either four or five handbreadths long (four for private houses, five for public buildings): these specifications give the best results as regards strength, durability and the appearance of both sides of the wall. He also mentions that in Spain and at Pitane in Asia Minor they made bricks of pumice which floated in water and were more resistant to damp.

2

Limestone

Stone was the standard material used for monumental buildings in Greece (3, 4).

In the Archaic period the first large stone temples were made of limestone, which is easily worked. Shell-limestone was used for the Temple of Zeus at Olympia. Local limestones were used for various other temples, such as that of Apollo Epikoureios at Bassai, and for the walls of cities and fortresses, as well as the foundations and other unseen parts of marble buildings.

3

Marble

In the Archaic period marble was used only on a limited scale in the Greek mainland: for some parts of the sixth-century Temple of Athena in Athens, for example, and for the facing of the Temple of Apollo at Delphi. However, it was much used for temples in the Cyclades, where it existed in abundance. Parian and Naxian marble, which was of very high quality, coarse-grained, easily carved and snow-white, was used mainly in sculpture.

In the Classical period marble came into widespread use with the large-scale exploitation of the quarries in Attica, especially those on Mt. Pentelikon. Pentelic marble is fine-grained and somewhat translucent but it contains particles of iron, which in time give it a slight reddish tinge. Most of the monumental edifices built in Athens in the fifth century B.C. were made of Pentelic marble; others were of marble from Agrileza (near Sounion) or Mt. Hymettos, or of a hard, dark limestone from Eleusis.

4

Many types of masonry, some of them very different from each other, were used in ancient Greece, mainly because the Greeks were always willing to try something new in search of improvements. The choice of one or another depended on the design of the building, the purpose for which it was to be used, the funds available, aesthetic considerations and the capabilities of the material. The main types of masonry (1) were:-

(a) Isodomic. The most commonly used in temples and other large buildings, consisting of rectangular blocks of uniform size laid in regular courses.

(b) Pseudo-isodomic. A modified form of the above, consisting of regular deep courses alternating with regular shallow ones.

(c) Trapezoidal. Used for fortification walls from the fourth century B.C. The blocks are laid in courses of uniform height but their sides are not vertical, so the visible face of each block is a trapezium.

3

4

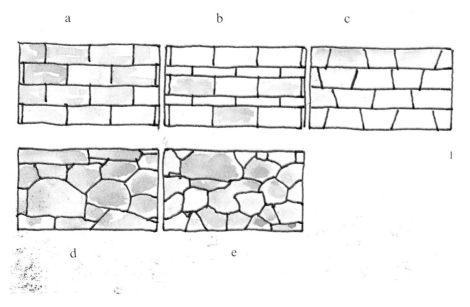

a   b   c

d   e

1

(d) Polygonal. Large cut blocks of stone, of irregular shapes and sizes but exactly fitted together. Polygonal masonry was economical because it reduced wastage to the minimum. It was used mainly for retaining walls and fortifications.

(e) Lesbian. Most commonly used in the Archaic period, chiefly for retaining walls. The joints are curvilinear but the blocks are still exactly fitted together, giving the wall greater strength. Difficult and expensive to make, but attractive in appearance.

(f) Rubble masonry. Stones of assorted shapes and sizes, usually unhewn or very roughly shaped. Used in all periods, mainly for low-cost work where quality is not important.

Mortar

Mortar was widely used in ancient Greek architecture, not so much as a binding agent but as a covering for floors (either on its own or as a bedding for mosaics) (2), for the walls and ceilings of houses, and also for the walls, columns and other architectural members of monumental buildings, especially those made of limestone. Great care was taken to face the floors and walls of cisterns with impermeable mortar, to make them watertight. The main ingredients used in making mortar were lime, gypsum, sea sand, pumice and powdered marble.

It was in the Roman period that mortar came into general use as a bond for masonry in all types of buildings. One type of masonry in which large quantities of mortar were used for bonding was called *opus caementicium* (from *caementum*, quarry stone or stone chippings): hence the modern meaning of the word "cement".

Metal

Metal was not much used in ancient architecture: apart from iron and bronze balustrades, it was chiefly used for door accessories (locks, hinges, etc.), doornails and the bronze facings often attached to doors. In monumental buildings the masonry was held together with iron cramps or dowel-pins coated with lead. Lead was also used for water pipes. Precious metals were sometimes used, but sparingly: certain parts of architectural members – such as the "eyes" at the centre of the volutes of an Ionic capital, or ornaments in the coffers of temple ceilings – might be made of (or merely covered with) gold or silver foil.

2

For a public building, the architect was required to specify in advance the kind of stone to be used and also the number of building blocks of each size and type that would be required. The ancient Greeks were very particular about choosing the right kind of stone and never wasted any of it (1).

Quarrying

As soon as an order for building stone was received, the quarry started extracting the stone and cutting it into blocks of the required size. The work was done by skilled craftsmen, usually slaves, in the way described below.

First of all, grooves were cut with saws or picks all round the piece of rock that was to be extracted. Then wooden wedges were inserted into the grooves and soaked with water so that they swelled up and split the rock into a chunk of exactly the right size. This method was used both for rectangular wall blocks and for cylindrical column drums. When monolithic columns were required, as in the case of a temple at Selinous, each cylindrical block of stone was extracted in one piece by cutting circular grooves in either the horizontal or the vertical plane, depending on the texture and grain of the rock. Every block was deliberately cut a few centimetres too large in all directions, to be trimmed on arrival at the site, so that any superficial damage occurring during transportation would not affect the appearance of the finished article.

1

2

Land transport

Transporting building stone from the quarry to the site was a slow and hazardous business, and extremely hard work. When the quarry was a long way away (those on Mt. Pentelikon, for example, are a good ten miles from the Acropolis), the journey took a full day, or even two for exceptionally heavy blocks. Further difficulties arose, of course, if there were hills or rough ground to be covered or if the stone had to be brought by sea.

Small blocks presented no problem: they were carried in carts drawn by oxen or mules. For transporting the bigger pieces, which often weighed many tons, various methods were devised. The commonest was to load the stone on to a wooden pallet or sledge, which was sometimes called a *chelone* (tortoise). If the ground was fairly flat, the pallet was pulled on wooden rollers by a large number of draught animals: the figure of 100 pairs of oxen is frequently mentioned in inscriptions. Where the route was downhill, as on Mt. Pentelikon, the pallet was allowed to slide down under its own weight, without rollers, and was kept under control by two ropes wound round tree-trunks or stout wooden stakes that were firmly wedged into square holes cut in the rock (2). The usual way of transporting very long pieces of stone (such as marble roof beams) was to rest them on the axles of specially-made carriages or, better still, to sling them beneath the axles with ropes or chains so that they would not be damaged by the inevitable jolts and bumps when travelling over rough ground.

Carriage by sea

By sea, building stone was generally carried in boats. Particularly large blocks were suspended between the hulls of two boats from a strong wooden beam fixed athwartships to form a sort of catamaran, slung low enough to be completely submerged so as to reduce the displacement of the boats (3).

Freight charges

Transporting quarry stone was a very costly business, especially overland. Ancient inscriptions tell us how the column drums for the portico of the Telesterion at Eleusis were carried from Mt. Pentelikon to their destination. For each drum, weighing about five tons, between 27 and 40 pairs of oxen were hired at a daily rate of over four drachmai per pair. Given a journey time of two or three days, the cost of transporting one column drum would have come to between 318 and 444 drachmai. To put this in context, the average daily wage in Athens at the end of the fifth century was one drachma. That so many oxen should have been required is not really surprising. Given that each pair could haul a load of up to 900 kg. and that the distance from Pentelikon to Eleusis is about 40 km., on bad roads and over rough, hilly ground, it is reasonable to assume that the oxen worked in relays rather than all at once. Transporting limestone from Corinth to Delphi was an equally costly undertaking. The first leg of the journey, from Corinth to Kirrha (the modern Itea) by sea, was not too expensive, but from there the stone had to be hauled up a steep mountainside to the sanctuary. The result was that the cost of a large block of limestone soared from 60 drachmai at the quarry to 240 drachmai – four times as much! – when freight charges were included.

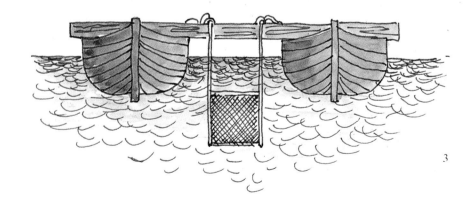

3

Once a block of stone had been cut, workmen at the quarry roughed it out with pointed hammers or picks into approximately the desired shape without too many irregularities or jagged edges. The final dressing process at the building site was usually carried out in two stages. In the first stage, which took place either in the sheds where the stonemasons had their workshops or (weather permitting) under awnings out of doors, the finishing touches were put to all the surfaces that would be hidden when they were in position in the building. Surfaces that would be visible were left partly-dressed in the first stage, to be finished only when the whole building was complete.

Tools and instruments

Our knowledge of the tools used by ancient stonemasons comes mainly from illustrations of them in works of art, supplemented by the inferences drawn from the marks left on building stones and comparison with masons' hand tools of our own time, from which they are unlikely to have differed much (1). They were all made of iron, unlike those of the prehistoric era, which were of bronze. Usually they were the property of the building contractor, who would give his workmen several sets of tools so that, when some were blunted by use and needed sharpening, work could proceed without interruption. The contractor paid to have them sharpened. Besides their stone-working tools, masons used various other instruments and accessories: squares, measuring-rods, crowbars, compasses, dividers, plumb-lines and so on. Numerous examples have been found in archaeological excavations and there are many illustrations of them, mostly on stelai marking the graves of stonemasons (2).

2

1

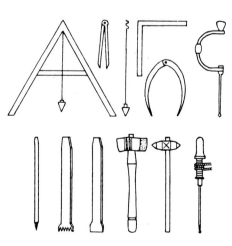

Machinery

Once the first stage of the final dressing process was completed, the stone was ready to be laid in position in the building. If it was small enough to be lifted by one or two men there was no problem, of course, but the bigger and heavier stones – especially the wall blocks and column drums of temples – were a different matter.

At least as early as the Archaic period, the Greeks are known to have used lifting devices which they had invented themselves or copied from neighbouring peoples (5). These precursors of the modern crane were used, among other things, for hoisting the actor who was often lowered from the heavens into the action of a play as a *deus ex machina* to resolve the plot. The Greeks, incidentally, used the word *geranos* in both senses of the English word "crane": probably the lifting device was so called because it was thought to resemble the bird.

Ancient cranes consisted of one or more long wooden booms controlled by ropes and iron pulley-blocks. Different types of crane were called by different names (*dispaston*, *pentaspaston*, *polyspaston*, etc.), the numerical prefix in each case denoting the arrangement of the pulleys (3). Information about the way they worked is provided by ancient writers and also by sculptural representations of lifting machines on monuments, mainly from the Roman period. One particularly interesting Roman relief (4) depicts a type of crane used for very heavy loads, powered by a treadmill operated by slaves.

3

4

5

Lifting

Stone blocks were lifted with strong ropes. If they were very heavy, the problem was to find a way of securing them so that they could be lifted with maximum convenience and minimum risk of accident. The ancient Greeks devised several safe methods of attaching heavy loads to the crane (3) in such a way that the marks made on the stone would either be hidden when the block was in place or else could be removed when the wall or column was finally dressed. One way, in use in the Archaic period (e.g. at Olympia and Delphi), was to make a U-shaped borehole down through the middle of the block from the upper surface, through which a loop of rope could be threaded (3). Another method devised later was to cut a U-shaped open groove at each end of a block (5), as at Aphaia (Aigina) and Akragas (Sicily): the grooves would of course be hidden when the blocks were laid end to end. In the Classical period various kinds of iron claws or tongs were used: one type was called a "crab" and another a "wolf".

Lugs

Another method that was much more widely used, especially for column drums, was to leave lugs projecting on the vertical faces of the stone to be lifted. Ropes were looped round the lugs to lift the stone into place, and once it was in position the lugs could be trimmed off. In many ancient buildings that were not completed, such as the Propylaia on the Athens Acropolis, the lugs were never removed (1).

Cramps and dowels

The limestone or marble masonry of monumental buildings (such as public buildings and temples) was not bonded with mortar like the smaller stones or bricks of private houses. First of all they were dressed so as to fit together perfectly, which helped to keep them in place, and then they were fastened to all the adjacent blocks (above, below and on each side) with metal cramps (2), usually made of bronze or iron. After insertion in the sockets cut for them in the stones, the cramps were coated with molten lead, partly in order to ensure a tight fit and partly to protect them against damp.
Iron or bronze dowels of rectangular section, again coated with lead, were used in addition to cramps for vertical joints.

1

2

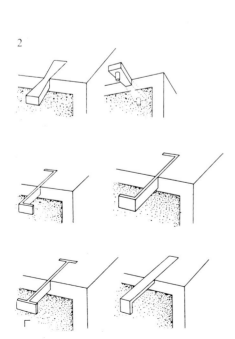

Empolia

Column drums were held together not with cramp-irons but with a device known as an *empolion*. This was a square block of wood embedded in the centre of the drum's upper or lower surface, which held the wooden centring pin or *polos* (4). In this way each drum could be rotated as it was lowered into position, until it was exactly aligned with the one below.

The use of empolia helped to protect buildings against earthquake damage, as is proved by the way so many temples have remained standing through the ages. It is also interesting to note that the wooden empolia and centring pins of the Parthenon have been preserved in excellent condition, because their position in the centre of the columns has kept them out of contact with the atmosphere.

5

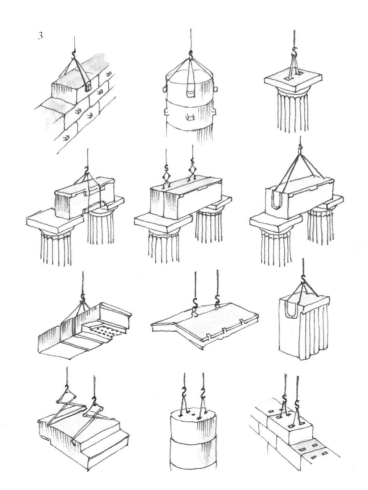

3

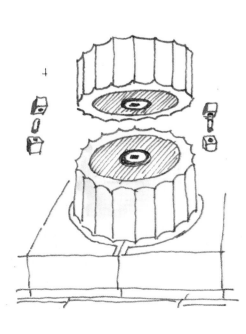

4

RESTORATION OF RUINED BUILDINGS

Since the 1980s the Acropolis has looked like nothing so much as a modern building site. A huge crane broods in the Parthenon, buildings are enveloped in scaffolding, blocks of stone are being moved from place to place, the site teems with labourers, craftsmen, architects and engineers, and sheds used as temporary workshops have sprung up here and there (1).

All this activity dates back to the start of the Acropolis maintenance and restoration programme, for the sad fact is that these splendid monuments, which have survived the ravages of time and a troubled history for over 2,440 years, are now in grave danger from the folly of modern man. The Acropolis has suffered particularly badly, first from the many mistakes that were made when restoration work was done in the late nineteenth and early twentieth centuries, and now more than ever from atmospheric pollution, which in recent years has harmed the ancient monuments as much as it has plagued the inhabitants of Athens.

What is restoration?

The word "restoration", in its broadest sense, covers all work done on an old building for the purpose of conservation or improvement: among other things, this might include dismantling, rebuilding and reinforcing sections of masonry, doing everyday maintenance work, adapting the building for new uses and so on. In the narrower sense of the word, restoration means reconstructing an old building, or part of it, using pieces of the original fabric that have either collapsed or been taken away from the site.

Aims

The main aims of restoration work can be summed up as follows:-
1. To restore the fabric as fully as possible, so as to stimulate visitors' interest by helping them to visualize the building as it was originally.
2. To draw attention to the artistic merit and historical value of the ruins.
3. To improve the site by giving greater prominence to the dimension of height.
4. By rebuilding the upper courses of walls, or even restoring the roof, to protect the lower courses from the elements.
5. To eliminate the causes of structural damage.
6. To protect the building as far as possible from further damage, however caused.

2

The Venice Charter

Restoration is a tricky business, fraught with problems which have to be dealt with on a case-by-case basis according to the nature of the monument, special local conditions and many other factors. However, there are certain fundamental principles that should be observed in every restoration project. Agreement was reached on these principles in 1964 at an international conference of architects in Venice, where they were enshrined in a document known as the Venice Charter. They may be summarized as follows:-

1. No restoration work should be done until everything possible is known about the building and its original form has been established with absolute certainty.

2. Respect for the original form of the building should be the paramount consideration: simplifications, modifications or alterations that risk perverting the original form should be avoided.

3. The use of new architectural members should be kept to the absolute minimum: if used, they should blend harmoniously with the rest of the building and be clearly distinguishable from the original materials.

4. Exhaustive records (photographs, drawings, descriptions, etc.) should be kept before, during and after the restoration work.

5. Every action should be reversible, in other words capable of being undone without causing damage to the building.

Some major restorations

Other sites in Greece where major restoration work has been done, besides the Acropolis in Athens, include the Temple of Aphaia on Aigina, the Temple of Poseidon at Sounion, the Treasury of the Athenians at Delphi, the Acropolis of Lindos on Rhodes, the theatre at Epidauros and the Odeion of Herodes Atticus in Athens. Two other "restored" buildings in Athens, the Stoa of Attalos and the Panathenaic Stadium, have actually been reconstructed from scratch, using a great deal of new material, but with scrupulous respect for the original design specifications. Several temples in southern Italy and Sicily have been lovingly restored, notably at Poseidonia (Paestum), Egesta (2), Selinous and Akragas.

ARCHITECTURAL DRAWINGS

Before construction work is started on a new project nowadays, the architect prepares a set of drawings to give an impression of what the finished building will look like and to help the builders by showing them all the design details as well as the proportions, in which the beauty of a building chiefly lies. These drawings are all done to scale. An architect makes a similar set of measured drawings, depicting the subject from all angles, before starting to restore an ancient building or attempting to reconstruct its original appearance.

Elevation

First and foremost among the drawings is the front elevation, a picture of the façade of the building. An elevation is a two-dimensional horizontal view from the front, back (rear elevation) or either side (side elevation), showing height and breadth only. Depth is completely ignored: there is no perspective, no hint of what lies behind the visible exterior (1, 2).

Plan

An important architectural aid, essential both to the builders of a new building and to archaeologists making measured drawings of an ancient one, is the plan (3), a plane drawing of a building (or part of a building) as viewed from above. A plan can be drawn not only at ground level but at any level above or below it, for the term covers any drawing that shows the layout of structural elements such as walls and columns on a horizontal plane: it is, in fact, a horizontal section (see next).

1

3

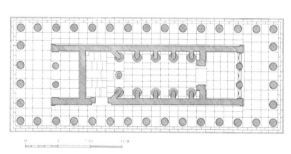

2

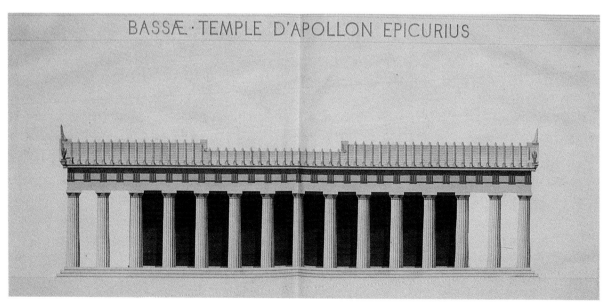

Vertical section

Another kind of architectural drawing in common use is the vertical section. A section literally means a cut, and a vertical section in this sense is a plane drawing of the surface that would be exposed if one were to make a vertical cut through the whole or part of a building, showing such structural details as the thickness of the roof, the roof supports, the thickness of the walls and so on. Any number of vertical sections can be made, taken through different parts of the building and at different angles, usually transverse (4) or longitudinal (5). Nowadays it is usual for an architect to take a number of sections, to make it easier for him to study the proportions and explain what he wants to the builders.

Perspective

A perspective drawing gives a three-dimensional view of the building and shows two or three sides simultaneously.

4

Axonometric

An axonometric drawing gives a three-dimensional view in a different projection, with the walls cut away to reveal the interior of the building and hidden structural details (6). It differs from the perspective drawing in that all lines are drawn exactly to scale and all parallel lines remain parallel, so that it appears distorted.

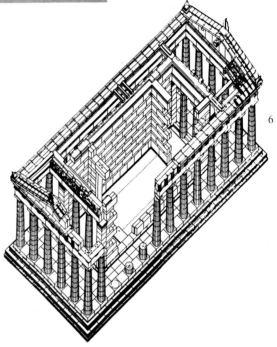

6

5

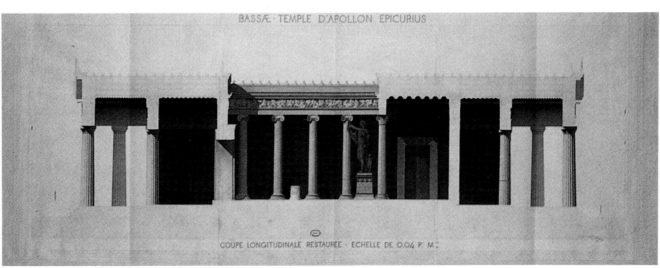

SOURCES

Our knowledge of ancient architecture owes much to the writings of ancient authors – not only those who wrote about buildings as such (e.g. Pausanias in his *Description of Greece* or Vitruvius in his *De Architectura*) but also those who provide incidental information about buildings in non-architectural works (e.g. Homer, Thucydides, Xenophon, Aristophanes). All of them have contributed to the history of architecture by identifying buildings or supplying additional particulars of known buildings.

Palaces

Then they ushered the newcomers into the royal buildings. Telemachus and his friend opened their eyes in wonder at all they saw as they passed through the king's palace. It seemed to them that this lofty hall of the sublime Menelaus was lit by something of the sun's splendour or the moon's. When they had feasted their eyes on the sight, they went and bathed in polished baths.

Odyssey IV. 40

Agora

As soon as the fresh Dawn had decked herself in crimson, the divine King Alcinous left his bed and conducted Odysseus, the royal sacker of cities, who had risen at the same time, to the place by the ships where the Phaeacians held their Assemblies; and there they sat down side by side on seats of polished marble. In the meantime Pallas Athene, pursuing her plans for the heroic Odysseus' return, went up and down the town disguised as a herald from the wise prince Alcinous. She accosted each of the Counsellors and gave them all this message: "Captains and Counsellors of the Phaeacians, follow me to the Assembly, where you shall hear about the stranger who has just arrived at our wise prince's palace. He has wandered all over the seas, and he looks like an immortal god."

Odyssey VIII. 1-15

Propylaia

The gateway [to the Acropolis] has a roof of white marble, and down to the present day it is unrivalled for the beauty and size of its stones.... On the left of the gateway is a building with pictures. Among those not effaced by time, I found Diomedes taking the [statue of] Athena from Troy, and Odysseus in Lemnos taking away the bow of Philoctetes.

Pausanias I. 22. 4, 6

The Athens Agora

Here stands Zeus, called Zeus of Freedom, and the Emperor Hadrian, a benefactor to all his subjects and especially to the city of the Athenians. A portico is built behind with pictures of the gods called the Twelve.

Pausanias I. 3. 2-3

Eponymous heroes

Before the meeting of the Assembly any Athenian who wishes shall write down the laws proposed by him and exhibit the same in front of the Eponymous Heroes.... Whosoever proposes a new statute shall write it on a white board and exhibit it in front of the Heroes on every day until the meeting of the Assembly.

Demosthenes XXIV. 23

Fortification walls

In this way the Athenians fortified their city in a very short time. Even today one can see that the building was done in a hurry. The foundations are made of different sorts of stone, sometimes not shaped so as to fit, but laid down just as each was brought up at the time; there are many pillars taken from tombs and fragments of sculpture mixed in with the rest. For the city boundaries were extended on all sides, and so in their haste they used everything that came to hand, sparing nothing. Themistocles also persuaded them to complete the walls of Piraeus, which had been begun previously during his year of office as archon.

Thucydides I. 93

The stadium at Olympia

At the end of the statues erected from athletes' penalties is what they call the hidden entrance, through which the Greek arbiters and the competitors enter the stadium. The stadium is a mound of earth, but it has a seat built for the presidents. Opposite the Greek arbiters is a white stone altar, and on this altar a woman sits and watches the Olympic games, the priestess of Demeter Chamyne (Demeter of the Ground), an office awarded by Elis to different women at different times.

Pausanias VI. 20. 8-9

Building contracts

Cities, as we know, when they give public notice of intent to let contracts for the building of temples or colossal statues, listen to the proposals of artists competing for the commission and bringing in their estimates and models, and then choose the man who will do the same work with the least expense and better than the others and more quickly.

Plutarch, *Moralia* 498E

Symmetry

There is nothing to which an architect should devote more thought than to the exact proportions of his building with reference to a certain part selected as the standard. After the standard of symmetry has been determined, and the proportionate dimensions adjusted by calculations, it is next the part of wisdom to consider the nature of the site, or questions of use or beauty, and modify the plan by diminutions or additions in such a manner that these diminutions or additions in the symmetrical relations may be seen to be made on correct principles, and without detracting at all from the effect.

Vitruvius VI.2.1

Colour

As for colours, some are natural products found in fixed places, and dug up there, while others are artificial compounds of different substances treated and mixed in proper proportions so as to be equally serviceable....

Quicksilver is useful for many purposes. For instance, neither silver nor copper can be gilded properly without it. And when gold has been woven into a garment, and the garment becomes worn out with age so that it is no longer respectable to use, the pieces of cloth are put into earthen pots, and burned up over a fire. The ashes are then thrown into water and quicksilver added thereto. This attracts all the bits of gold, and makes them combine with itself. The water is then poured off, and the rest emptied into a cloth and squeezed in the hands, whereupon the quicksilver, being a liquid, escapes through the loose texture of the cloth, but the gold, which has been brought together by the squeezing, is found inside in a pure state.

Vitruvius VII.6.1, VII.8.4

Purple dye

I shall now begin to speak of purple, which exceeds all the colours that have so far been mentioned both in costliness and in the superiority of its delightful effect. It is obtained from a marine shellfish, from which is made the purple dye, which is as wonderful to the careful observer as anything else in nature; for it has not the same shade in all the places where it is found, but is naturally qualified by the course of the sun. That which is found in Pontus and Gaul is black, because those countries are nearest to the north. As one passes on from north to west, it is found of a bluish shade. Due east and west, what is found is of a violet shade. That

which is obtained in southern countries is naturally red in quality, and therefore this is found in the island of Rhodes and in other such countries that are nearest to the course of the sun.

Vitruvius VII.13.1-2

ANCIENT GREEK TEMPLES AND OTHER MONUMENTAL BUILDINGS

Doric

Date	Name	Place	Date	Name	Place
7th c.	of Apollo Ismenios	Thebes	460	of Poseidon	Poseidonia (Paestum)
640	of Apollo	Thermon	460	of Juno Lacinia	Akragas
640	of Athena Pronaia	Delphi	460	Temple A	Selinous
600	of Apollo	Cyrene	450-425	of Apollo	Bassai
600	of Artemis	Kerkyra (Corfu)	449-444	of Hephaistos	Athens
590	of Hera	Olympia	447-432	Parthenon	Athens
580	Tholos (old)	Delphi	444-440	of Poseidon	Sounion
575	of Artemis	Syracuse	440-436	of Ares	Athens
575	of Olympian Zeus	Syracuse	437-432	Propylaia	Athens
555-530	Temple C	Selinous	436-432	of Nemesis	Rhamnous
550	of Apollo Daphnephoros	Eretria	430	of Concord	Akragas
540	of Athena	Assos	425-417	of Apollo (of the Athenians)	Delos
540	Apollo	Corinth	424-416	temple	Egesta
535	Temple D	Selinous	423-416	of Hera (new)	Argive Heraion
530	"Basilica"	Poseidonia (Paestum)	390	of Amphiaraos	Oropos
525	Temple FS	Selinous	390	of Artemis	Epidauros
529-515	Peisistratid Temple of Athena	Athens	380	of Asklepios	Epidauros
520-450	of Apollo ("GT")	Selinous	366-326	of Apollo	Delphi
510	of Olympian Zeus	Akragas	350	of Athena Alea	Tegea
510	of Demeter	Poseidonia (Paestum)	340	of Zeus	Nemea
507	Treasury of the Athenians	Delphi	321	of Zeus	Stratos
500	"Tavole Paladine"	Metapontion	320	Metroön	Olympia
500	of Athena Pronaia	Delphi	280	Arsinoeion	Samothrake
495-485	of Aphaia	Aigina	250	of Athena Polias	Pergamon
490-480	Old Parthenon	Athens	180	of Despoina	Lykosoura
480	of Athena	Syracuse	170	of Dionysos	Pergamon
460	of Zeus	Olympia	150	of Hera Basileia	Pergamon
			A.D. 125	of Artemis Propylaia	Eleusis

Ionic

Date	Name	Place	Date	Name	Place
565	of Apollo	Naukratis	340-156	of Athena Polias	Priene
560-540	of Artemis (old)	Ephesos	356-236	of Artemis (new)	Ephesos
530	of Hera	Samos	350-300	of Artemis-Kybele	Sardis
530	Treasury		313-41	of Apollo	Didyma
	of the Massiliotes	Delphi	280	of Aphrodite	Messa, Lesvos
450-425	temple	Locri Epizephyrii	193	of Dionysos	Teos
449	by the Ilissos	Athens	175	of Artemis	
427-424	Athena Nike	Athens		Leukophryene	Magnesia
421-405	Erechtheion	Athens			ad Maeandrum
355-350	Mausoleum	Halikarnassos	A.D. 125	of Aphrodite	Aphrodisias
			A.D. 125	of Zeus	Aizanoi

While they proceed, all turns to melody
The columned shaff the very triglyph, rings
Yea, I believe that all the temple sings

Goette, *Faust 6446*

GLOSSARY

acropolis: a hilltop citadel.

agora: the commercial and civic centre of an ancient Greek city.

Amazonomachy: the victorious battle of the Athenians under Theseus against the invading Amazons.

antefix: an ornament at the edge of a roof, concealing the ends of the tiles.

Archaic period: *c.* 700-480 B.C.

archons: in Classical Athens, the nine supreme officers of state, elected annually. One of them, the Eponymous Archon, gave his name to the year in which he held office.

barrel-vault: a vault of semicircular section forming a hemicylindrical roof.

Boule: Administrative Council or Senate.

bouleuterion: the meeting-place of the Boule of a city, sanctuary, etc.

cavea: the concave seating area of an ancient theatre (also called **koilon**).

cella: the principal chamber of a temple containing the cult statue of the god or goddess (also called **sekos**).

Centauromachy: the fighting between Lapiths and Centaurs at the wedding of the Lapith king Peirithoös.

choregos (or choragos): the sponsor of a theatrical production. Hence **choregic (or choragic) monument**.

chryselephantine: consisting of an inner core of wood with an outer covering of gold and ivory.

Cyclopean masonry: huge boulders, roughly worked and irregular in shape, with small stones filling the gaps.

Ekklesia: Assembly of the People.

frieze: the horizontal band above the architrave of a temple. In the Doric order it consisted of alternating triglyphs and metopes (qq.v.); in the Ionic order it was a continuous band of reliefs, usually illustrating a narrative.

Gigantomachy: the battle between the Gods and the Giants.

Hellenistic period: 323-146 B.C.

hero: a person of superhuman powers, venerated after his death (often locally) as an immortal demigod; **heroön:** a shrine or memorial to a hero.

hypostyle: having interior columns to support the roof.

intercolumniation: the distance between the centre of one column and the centre of the next.

kore (pl. korai): an Archaic statue of a young woman.

kouros (pl. kouroi): an Archaic statue of a young man.

naiskos: a small temple, or a monument (e.g. a tombstone) resembling a temple.

order: a style of architecture (the principal ones in ancient Greece being the Doric, Ionic and Corinthian) classified by the style of the columns and entablature.

peplos: a draped outer robe, worn usually by women. A specially embroidered peplos was carried in procession and dedicated to Athena at the Great Panathenaia festival.

peristyle: a colonnade round a building or courtyard. So **peristyle courtyard:** a courtyard with a colonnaded gallery along all four sides.

propylaia: a monumental entrance grander and architecturally more complex than a propylon.

propylon: a monumental gateway into a sanctuary, etc.

Roman period: in Greece, 146 B.C. to A.D. 267.

sekos: the temple building proper, excluding porches, etc. If it consists of a single room, it is the same as the **cella**.

sima: the terracotta or marble gutter of a building, on the gables and sometimes along the sides.

stadion or stade: a unit of length equal to 600 feet (*podes*), varying from one part of Greece to another (from 177.50 to 192.28 metres); the basic unit of distance for foot-races. Hence the word *stadion* (stadium) was used for the building where such races were run.

stele (pl. stelai): an upright stone slab or tablet.

stoa: a colonnaded gallery or portico.

tholos: a rotunda; **tholos tomb:** a "beehive" tomb, i.e. a round, vaulted burial chamber.

treasury: a building resembling a small temple, used for the safe keeping of valuable offerings in a sanctuary.

tyrant: an absolute ruler, not necessarily a tyrant in the modern sense.

BIBLIOGRAPHY

For general information on the history of Greek architecture see:
J.J. Coulton, *Ancient Greek Architects at Work* (1977),
W.B. Dinsmoor, *The Architecture of Ancient Greece* (3rd ed., 1975),
École National Supérieure des Beaux-Arts, *Paris-Rome-Athènes* (exhibition catalogue) (1982),
A.W. Lawrence, *Greek Architecture* (1957),
D.S. Robertson, *A Handbook of Greek and Roman Architecture* (1964),
R. Scranton, *Greek Architecture* (1967),
R.V. Schroder, *Ancient Greece from the Air* (1974).

On city planning there are two monumental standard works:
W. Hoepfner and E.L. Schwandner, *Haus und Stadt im klassischen Griechenland* (1986),
R. Martin, *L'urbanisme dans la Grèce antique* (1956),
as well as a less exhaustive work in English:-
R.E. Wycherley, *How the Greeks Built Cities* (2nd ed., 1976).

On building materials and construction methods:
R. Martin, *Manuel d'architecture grecque*, I: *Matériaux et techniques* (1965),

W. Müller-Wiener, *Griechisches Bauwesen in der Antike* (1988).

Or, for a very brief review of the subject:
J.M. Camp and W.B. Dinsmoor, *Ancient Athenian Building Methods* (1984) in the series "Excavations of the Athenian Agora Picture Books", published by the American School of Classical Studies in Athens.
On materials and methods in use in the Roman period:-
J.P. Adam, *La Construction Romaine. Matériaux et techniques* (1984).

On the quarrying, transportation and preparation of building stone:
M. Korres, *From Pentelicon to the Parthenon* (1995).

The following books on the Acropolis restoration programme, besides being essential reading on that particular subject, also contain a wealth of information about ancient Greek architecture in general:-
R. Economakis (ed.), *Acropolis Restoration: The CCAM Intervention* (1994),
P. Tournikiotis (ed.), *The Parthenon and its Impact in Modern Times* (1994).

ILLUSTRATIONS

Mosaic". Iraklion Museum.
4. Clay model of a two-storey house at Arkhanes, Crete. 1600 B.C. Iraklion Museum.
5. The excavated settlement at Akrotiri, Thera: the West House. 16th cent. B.C. Photo: Ch. Doumas.

THE *POLIS* AND CITY PLANNING SYSTEMS, pp. 22-23
1. Plan of Athens in the 5th cent. B.C. Drawn by J. Travlos.
2. Plan of Priene in the late 4th cent. B.C. Drawn by A. von Gerkan.

PLANNING AND ROAD-BUILDING, pp. 24-25
1. The great stone-paved road from the agora of ancient Corinth to Lechaion.
2. The bridge over the Eleusinian Kephisos.
3. A milestone of the 2nd cent. A.D. Athens, Epigraphical Museum.

ANCIENT GREEK HOUSES, pp. 26-27
1. Courtyard of a house at Priene, Asia Minor. Drawing by S. Zarambouka, after a reconstruction by F. Krischen (1912).
2. Courtyard of a house at Olynthos. Drawing by S. Zarambouka, after a reconstruction by D. Robinson.
3. Axonometric reconstruction drawing of a typical ancient Greek house. Drawn by S. Zarambouka.

HOUSES FOR DIFFERENT CLIMATES AND LIFESTYLES, pp. 28-29
1, 2, 3. Houses in Athens (1), at Vari (2) and on Delos (3). Drawings by S. Zarambouka, based on reconstructions.
4. Isometric drawing of a housing block in Piraeus. Reconstruction by W. Hoepfner and E.L. Schwandner.
5. Reconstruction drawing of the House of Dionysos at Pella, by E. Yiouri.

ARCHITECTURAL AND DECORATIVE ELEMENTS, pp. 30-31
1, 2. Mosaic floors from houses on Delos. 2nd cent. B.C.
3, 4. Laconian and Corinthian tiling.
5. Reconstruction drawing of the terracotta sima of the Middle Stoa in the Athens Agora. Mid 2nd cent. B.C. Athens, American School of Classical Studies.

DOORS AND WINDOWS, pp. 32-33
1. Picture of a door on the François Vase. 570 B.C. Drawing by S. Zarambouka.
2. A door in Kifissia, Athens. Photo: N. Kouskoleka.
3. Door and doorsill of a house at Olynthos. 5th-4th cent. B.C.
4. Picture of a window on a vase from southern Italy. 4th cent. B.C.
5. A window in the House of the Trident on Delos. 2nd cent. B.C.

THE AGORA, pp. 34-35
1. The agora at Assos. Drawing by S. Zarambouka, after the reconstruction by Clarke and Bacon.

STOAS: MULTI-PURPOSE BUILDINGS, pp. 36-37
1, 2, 3. General view, floor plan and interior of the Stoa of Attalos, 159-138 B.C.

THE PNYX, pp. 38-39
1. The Pnyx as it is today. In the centre is the speaker's rostrum carved out of the rock.

2. Model of the city of Athens, with the Pnyx near the bottom left-hand corner.

ADMINISTRATIVE BUILDINGS, pp. 40-41
1. Buildings in the S.W. corner of the Agora. Drawing by S. Zarambouka, after the reconstruction by J. Travlos.
2, 3, 4. Ground plans of the buildings in Fig. 1.
5. The Monument of the Eponymous Heroes. Drawing by S. Zarambouka, after the reconstruction by W.B. Dinsmoor.

LAW COURTS AND PRISONS, pp. 42-43
1. Jurors' voting discs inscribed ΨΗΦΟΣ ΔΗΜΟΣΙΑ ("Civic vote"). Athens, Agora Museum.
2. The Royal Stoa. Drawing by W.B. Dinsmoor, Jr. Athens, American School of Classical Studies.
3. Reconstruction of a building in the Agora as a prison, after J.E. Jones, with ground plan of the existing foundations. Drawing by S. Zarambouka.
4. Vases of the 3rd cent. B.C. Athens, Agora Museum.

THEATRES, pp. 44-45
1. The Theatre of Dionysos on the south slope of the Acropolis.
2. The theatre at Priene, Asia Minor, as it was in the late 2nd cent. B.C.
3. The theatre at Aspendos, Asia Minor. 4th cent. B.C.

ODEIA (CONCERT HALLS), pp. 46-47
1. Model of the Acropolis viewed from the south, with the Acropolis itself visible through the window behind it. Foreground, L. to R.: Odeion of Herodes Atticus, Stoa of Eumenes, Sanctuary and Theatre of Dionysos, Odeion of Perikles. Reconstruction by M. Korres. Photo: H.R. Goette.
2. Aerial view of the same model.
3. The Monument of Lysikrates.

LIBRARIES, pp. 48-49
1. Hadrian's Library (A.D. 132). Photograph; drawing by S. Zarambouka, based on a reconstruction.
2. Inscription from the Library of Pantainos (c. A.D. 100). Athens, Agora Museum.

GYMNASIA AND PALAISTRAI, pp. 50-51
1, 2. Model and ground plan of the gymnasium at Delphi, and photograph of the ruins.

STADIA AND HIPPODROMES, pp. 52-53
1. The Panathenaic Stadium in Athens, restored at the end of the 19th century.
2. The stadium at Nemea.
3. Plan of the hippodrome at Olympia.
4. Attic black-figure kylix with a painting of a chariot race. *Ca.* 550 B.C. Athens, National Archaeological Museum.

FACILITIES FOR TRAVELLERS AND PUBLIC HYGIENE, pp. 54-55
1. Plan of the *katagogion* at Epidauros.
2. The Pinakotheke in the Propylaia on the Athens Acropolis. Reconstruction drawing by J. Travlos.
3. Reconstruction drawing of a public toilet of the Roman period (detail).

"*Architecture depends on Order in Greek* τάξις,
Arrangement in Greek διάθεσις, *Eurythmy, Summetry,
Propriety, and Economy in Greek* οικονομία"

Vitruvius
Book 1 chap. II

Ioanna E. Phoca was born in Athens in 1939. She was educated at the American College of Greece and at Athens University, where she read Archaeology. She has worked on archaeological digs in Greece and was a member of the editorial team of the *Encyclopaedia Papyros Larousse Britannica*. Since 1988 she has written and translated a number of books on archaeology intended for a non-specialized readership and for young readers.

Panos D. Valavanis was born in Athens in 1954. After reading Archaeology at Athens University he went to Germany for postgraduate studies at the Archaeological Institute of Würzburg University. Since 1980 he has been working at Athens University, first as a research assistant, from 1988 to 1994 as a Reader and since 1994 as Assistant Professor of Classical Archaeology. His doctoral dissertation and most of his research papers have been on ancient Greek pottery and architecture, the topography of the ancient monuments in Athens and more recently on ancient Greek technology.

By the same authors:
1. ΤΑ ΑΓΓΕΙΑ ΚΑΙ Ο ΚΟΣΜΟΣ ΤΟΥΣ – Kedros 1990, 1992, 1997
Also published in English, German, French and Swedish editions as GREEK POTTERY, A CULTURE CAPTURED IN CLAY – Kedros 1992, 1996
DIE VASEN UND IHRE WELT – Kedros 1992
LE MONDE DES VASES GRECS – Kedros 1992, Kedros 1998
KERAMIKEN OCH DESS VÄRLD – Kedros 1992

2. ΑΡΧΙΤΕΚΤΟΝΙΚΗ ΚΑΙ ΠΟΛΕΟΔΟΜΙΑ – Kedros 1992, 1995, 1998, 2000
ARCHITECTURE AND CITY PLANNING – Kedros 1999, 2000, 2002

3. ΠΕΡΙΠΑΤΟΙ ΣΤΗΝ ΑΘΗΝΑ ΚΑΙ ΤΗΝ ΑΤΤΙΚΗ.
Τόποι, θεοί, μνημεία – Kedros 1994, 1995
Also published in English
ATHENS AND ATTICA ARCHAEOLOGICAL OUTINGS
History and myth, Gods and monuments,
Cite and Country – Kedros 1997

Forthcoming titles in the series "Rediscovering Ancient Greece":
4. ΑΓΑΛΜΑΤΑ ΚΑΙ ΓΛΥΠΤΕΣ (SCULPTURE AND SCULPTORS)
5. ΝΟΜΙΣΜΑΤΑ ΚΑΙ ΟΙΚΟΝΟΜΙΑ (COINS AND THE ECONOMY)

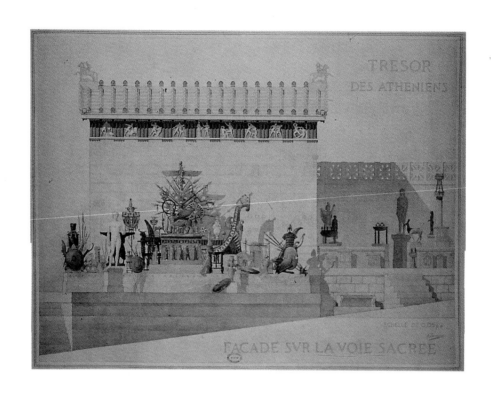

TYPESETTING AND COLOUR SEPARATIONS BY FOTOKYTTARO Ltd.
14 ARMODIOU St., ATHENS
FOR KEDROS BOOKS S.A.
3 GENNADIOU St., GR-106 78 ATHENS, TEL. 38 02 007
2002